AGAINST ALL ODDS

DANIEL CASAMASSA

To My Father

Losing him from my life was tragic. I was so weak after he died and still have tough days just thinking of him and the tragedy that occurred that day. He was my best friend who I leaned on for spiritual and financial help, among other things. I now feel obligated to take on his former role as "man of the house." With him gone, I cannot let him down, so I will work as hard as possible and love as much as possible until the day I die.

When I look back on his life and what he accomplished, he taught me how to live life the right way: look to serve others and help those in need. That is what I intend to do. I want to live the rest of my life in honor of him as he watches me from heaven go to work here on Earth. The thought of my father makes me weak, but at the same time, builds me up and gives me strength to persevere and work as hard as I possibly can each and every day.

Although I will have to wait until I meet my father again, I cannot be somber forever because that is not how he would want me to live my life. So, this book is dedicated to my father, and I promise to live an honorable life just like he did for 73 remarkable years.

CONTENTS

Acknowledgments

First and foremost, I want to thank God for saving me. I also want to thank my amazing family for sticking by me during the troubled times. My siblings never stopped believing in me. I also cannot forget about all my cousins, aunts, uncles, and grandparents on my mother's and father's side of the family. They are my inspiration, and I love them unconditionally.

Furthermore, I want to thank my camp friends and camp directors who always stood by my side, supported me, and made me laugh and enjoy life during four unforgettable years at Kenmont Camp in Kent, CT. Thank you, Tom, Scott, Howie, Markel, Noel, Jimmy, Jimmy M., Lucky, and all the others from around the world who inspired me to achieve greatness at camp. The great times we had will be cherished forever.

To my high school teacher, Mr. Aikin, who always believed in me, I will be forever thankful. He taught me how to become a great writer. Mr. Aikin, thanks for never giving up on me.

Next, I want to thank my Uncle Bobby and Uncle Billy for all their phone calls over the past few years since I lost my father. They have been like a counselor to me, and I will be forever grateful for having them both in my life.

I also want to thank my brother David, my mother, and my Aunt Annie who put in the time and looked over my book to help make this day possible. They are three of the smartest people I know. I also cannot forget about my amazing fifth graders who also looked over parts of my book, making sure it was free of grammatical errors before publication. They are truly unbelievable. Finally, I want to thank my best friend, my sister Christy, who designed the book cover. This beautiful design is just one of her many talents.

Thank you, Aunt Annie (and your family), for helping me out during my challenging times in high school. You and your family are so amazing, and I will always cherish the memorable times we had in your home in Queens when I was in high school. Thanks for all the hospitality and love you showed me. I am forever grateful.

I can't forget to give a shout out to my amazing Aunt Bea who has been a leader on my father's side of the family, and my wonderful Grandma Rosemary (rest in peace), who exemplified throughout her life what it means to love others. They both were always there for me when times were tough with words of wisdom and overflowing love. We need more kind, loving people in the world like them. They are truly special.

Lastly, I want to acknowledge my strong and amazing mother. She never stopped believing in me and always knew I would turn my life around and make it through on top. Mom, thank you for being there for me and helping me get through my days in school and beyond. Those days were tough, but you proved to be so much tougher. You are my saving grace.

FOREWORD

Against All Odds is a book about one man's journey toward becoming the incredible person that he is today. That man is my brother Daniel. One should never judge a book by its cover, and one should never judge a person based on one mistake, or a multitude of mistakes. Why is that? The answer to that question is simple: because one should not be judged based on their mistakes but rather how they respond to those mistakes and learn from them. A person's true character is revealed when you consider how they respond to their mistakes and the challenges they face in life. Life offers up countless challenges for each of us, and Daniel's life was no different. He was constantly forced to overcome both large and small obstacles but through strong will and an optimistic approach, he was able to persevere.

This book dives deep into Daniel's journey to show how one can and should respond to their own mistakes, but it also is an amazing testimony into what types of challenges can be overcome with a strong spirit of determination. Growing up with Daniel, you could tell he was someone that was thrown many curveballs in life but if you looked close enough, what you could also see was someone who was working through each and every one of them. Like with many people, growth does not happen overnight and that was the case for Daniel, but there came a point in his life where he woke up one day and never looked back. If you were to take a snapshot of Daniel's life every 5 years starting in his late teens, you would think that each person was someone completely different because the growth was dramatic and just continued to happen. How did Danny make this happen? The answer to this question is also very simple: perseverance.

My brother Daniel is one of the more unique and special people you will ever come across and the same can be said for his story. *Against All Odds* takes you through the story that is his life and keeps you amazed as to how one man could overcome so much and still end up where he is today. This book has me in tears every time I read it because not only are you reading about Daniel's journey, but also hidden within each word is the story of the pain and heartache he had to overcome to get to where he is today. After all is said and done, everything he went through made him into the man he is today and to me, that is someone I am lucky to have in my corner and that I am proud to call my brother!

David Casamassa

INTRODUCTION

When life throws challenges your way, you cannot just sit there waiting for things to happen. You need to stand up and initiate a positive change as if your life depended on it. You need to work as hard as possible, while persevering to get through the tough times. This book will take you on a journey into my childhood and high school days when I beat the odds and overcame all of life's adversity both emotionally and academically. My number one goal for this book is to influence and inspire those that are struggling in school and/or in life.

My hope is that after reading this book, you will learn that through hard work and perseverance, life's trials and tribulations can be overcome. This book is structured in a way that gives you a glimpse into each stage of my life, starting from birth. I will take you on an unforgettable journey and roller coaster ride that has lasted for three decades and counting. For the first time in my life, I have decided to go public in order to get many things off my chest. So sit back, relax, and enjoy the book.

ONE

And the Story Begins

My story began on January 19, 1985, in Queens, New York. I thank God for getting me through the early days of my life and for giving my mother the strength to first make it through the pregnancy and then to give birth without any major complications. I was truly blessed.

After a long day of tears, laughter, and sheer exhaustion, it was time to make the transition from the hospital to our home in Queens. My parents were relieved and happy to finally go home.

Things were starting to get crazy for my parents; I was their third child in the past four years. The oldest sibling was Mark, who turned 4 two days earlier on January 17, then Lauren, who was only 2 years old at the time. It was hectic for my mother at times, especially when she was home with the kids while my father was out working as a conductor on the Long Island Railroad supporting the family financially. Although it was challenging for my mother, this was nothing new for her; she was an experienced mother. Together my parents were able to successfully balance their work schedules with the duties and responsibilities that were required to take care of three children.

It was not long before my parents were once again welcoming another Casamassa into our family. Fourteen months after I came into this world, my mother was giving birth again. It was March 12, 1986, when my sister Christy was born. My parents were now dealing with two girls and two boys all in the same household with only five years separating us. Mark, now at age 5, was the veteran child around the house. Crying, screaming, and fighting were the norm during that year and for the next several years. When we were all grown up, our parents always reminded us that those days were "hectic and crazy," but they would not have traded them for the world.

During that challenging time, my parents learned how to work as a team and collaborate, while trying to meet and achieve one common goal: teaching us right from wrong. It is quite evident from praise they still get today and compliments they received during those years that they met and achieved their number one goal.

Over the next few years, my parents were getting acclimated to raising four young children. While my father was working tirelessly, my mother was working equally hard, helping us walk and talk while managing the daily schedules and all the various behaviors that we expressed as kids. My mother's academic background in education certainly came in handy.

Times were crazy and hectic in the Casamassa household during those early years, but the unconditional love my parents espoused helped them overcome all obstacles, as they worked together, relied on their faith, and exhibited a substantial amount of patience. That is not to say they did not fight, argue, and disagree because they were always quick to mention that they did indeed fight when we were younger. But most of all, they were able to throw their egos and differences aside and forgive each other, and most importantly, take ownership for their wrongdoings and move forward.

In 1988, a few months after I turned three, it seemed my parents were ready again to expand the family tree. They were ready to put on their winning uniforms and welcome a new life into the world. On March 1, 1988, my younger brother was born. The birth of David presented new challenges for my parents. There were now five kids, ranging in age from newborn to 7 years old, and two adults residing in a house that looked like it was getting smaller with each passing day. With my father continuing to juggle work and parenting, my mother's entire day was spent caring for and safeguarding five children.

This full-time occupation was done in an urban neighborhood that, at times, became understandably noisy. Not only were the noises of buses, trains, and neighbors outside the house hard to cope with for my parents, but also, I am sure the noises inside the house, were heard from a distance. The noise level in our home during the 1980s was undeniably loud, but in the 1990s, it only became louder.

The 1980s were fast paced and filled with many miracles, trials, and tribulations. But just when you thought my parents were content to live happily with their five children, they surprised us once again.

Maria Grace was born on October 4, 1990. My father called home to happily announce this wonderful news. My grandma was ecstatic. She was literally pacing around the house joyfully singing the popular "Brady Bunch" song, symbolizing the number of kids now in the family: three boys and three girls. We were so happy and could not wait to see Maria Grace.

This completed our family tree. This was our parents' sixth and final child together over a ten-year span. Not only would this life-changing event impact them financially, but it also was starting to take a toll on them physically and emotionally.

In March of 1991, my father had just turned 49. He was now a conductor for more than 24 years on the L.I.R.R. During that year, my father was dealing with a potentially dangerous heart condition that posed an imminent threat to his life. Although those conditions were present and ominous, he was ready to beat the odds and take care of his six children with my mother.

My mother was also dealing with her own physical issues at the time. After turning 36, she was diagnosed with cervical cancer. The cancer did not deter or discourage my mother from following her dreams, though. Eventually, with God's healing hand and the expertise of doctors, the cancer subsided. My parents were not planning on having any more children, but that condition effectively ended all their future chances of giving birth to another child.

My mother described the feeling of giving birth: "It was the worst pain I have ever felt in my life, very excruciating." She felt that same excruciating pain six times in her life, and she also dealt with the physical and mental toll of one miscarriage. With that said, my mother felt blessed and content with the family she had.

During those early years, times were hard financially, but my parents always seemed to stay optimistic no matter what. Trying to pay the bills and provide for six children was difficult for them, to say the least, but donations and help from family members, friends, and our local church with bags of clothing and other valuable resources were a blessing. Those significant contributions helped my parents use their own money to help pay off some bills and put gas in our one and only family car.

Our church at the time, the Church of the Nazarene, located in Queens, New York, was one of many sources who donated clothing and supported our family during times of need. I was always told that it was better to give than receive. My parents felt an obligation to give back to the church that was so kind and giving to our family during those tough times. They helped out where it was needed in the small church by joining the choir and teaching classes.

Another generous financial supporter for us was our mother's extended family. Her family was always quick to give without expecting anything in return. My mother's four brothers and two sisters showed tons of support and were always quick to donate clothing and other valuables.

My parents also had the benefit of loyal and giving friends helping them out financially. Their friends helped and provided them with the necessities needed to survive and care for six needy children. My mother and father told me that they remembered times when they would walk outside the front door and find big black bags on our stoop filled with clothing, hats, gloves, and coats. These items were desperately needed and beneficial to us, especially during the frigid nights of winter.

Even the clothes that did not fit us became useful, using them for sleepwear or to lounge in and relax. Sometimes we would use our clothing as window shades to fight off the bright sun that beamed in through our porch windows. We had to be creative and help our parents save money in any way that we could. We were grateful to have family and friends that were willing to donate and ease our financial burdens.

As for our home in Queens, it was a three-story house, but all the rooms were small, and some of the rooms like our kitchen, had holes/crawl spaces that ran through the entire room. I remember countless times playing hide-and-seek with my siblings in the house and using the holes and crawl spaces in the kitchen and other rooms to hide, but only to find raccoons, mice, etc. in them while hiding. The unfinished basement in our home also had frequent visitors from wildlife, especially at the back of the basement in a pitch-dark room, which frightened almost anyone who dared to walk in it.

When it came to health care, the New York City Board of Health helped to alleviate the medical costs for our large family. We were eligible to be covered under the Wic Program because my sister Christy and I were diagnosed with lead poisoning. The lead poisoning was a consequence of my father burning off house paint when we were home. He told me that neither of us reacted physically to the exposure, but the tests still came back positive. The Wic Program, similar to the Food Stamp Program, assists struggling families with their medical needs.

At the time my mother was pregnant, and some of us were under the age of 5, which were two important qualifications for program eligibility. My parents' low-income level further strengthened our case for public assistance. After meeting the necessary requirements, our family received vital health care when we needed it most.

Those early days were challenging for us, but we managed well and used literally anything and everything to get by. I remember during the winter seasons we would go to Forest Park in Queens and go down this big hill sledding during the snowy days using garbage pail covers. Yes, you read that right: garbage pail covers! I must add that they were quite effective, too.

To continue the point of using what was available, we used big pieces of plywood to create the backboard for our basketball hoop. Additionally, we utilized tape to make the square on the backboard to complete the professional look. It was a functional basketball hoop that provided hours of fun, but it was certainly not a traditional one by any stretch of the imagination.

When times are tough, even at a young age, you learn to be thankful for what you have. For the most part, we were thankful as kids. Since space was limited in our house filled with eight people, we learned to work together. Eight people in one house had its pros and cons, but if you asked each of us now, we would not have wanted it any differently. Everyone experiences hardships at different points in their lives, but it is how you respond to those tough times that will determine your ability to get through it and succeed.

Finding comfort and love from my family helped me get through all the tough times. In the next chapter you will learn about the unique pros and cons that I experienced living with seven other people in one house.

<u>An Inspirational Quote for You</u>

"Home sweet home. This is the place to find happiness. If one
does not find it here, one does not find it anywhere."

– M. K. Soni

For my family and me growing up during those early years, the experiences we
had are now cherished. Our home was not always perfect, but our unconditional love helped pave the way and create happiness in it. Everyone has a family and looks for love; for myself, I always looked home for love and found it.

I believe anyone who is in need of love and affection can always find it at
home from their family. If not at home, then possibly at another close relative's
house or a friend who you are close with and consider family. Most importantly, try finding someone who you can put your trust and faith in.

TWO

Eight in One

When Maria Grace was born, it was official: Eight people were now living in one house. Living with seven other people under one roof for me was fun and at times stressful, but truthfully, the good times outweighed the bad. I believe every situation in life has its ups and downs, and of course the good times are easy to get through, but it is the challenging times that can be difficult to overcome. One change that brought both benefits and difficulties was when my mother home-schooled all of us simultaneously.

Home-schooling was a choice my mother made, and it came with many challenges. My mother used her experience and expertise in education, along with her faith, to give us an optimal learning environment. It was easier to home-school us when my father was home, but most of the time he was fulfilling his work obligations. My mother officially taught five of us, with Maria Grace later having her academic experience in a public school.

My mother took on the task to educate us and to provide us with the necessary tools needed to flourish and succeed academically. In organizing a daily schedule, my mother utilized the various rooms on the first floor of our home to facilitate snack and lunch times, and even "recess." The kitchen was the designated cafeteria, while the porch and backyard were used when we had "recess" or when we earned a break. It was quite structured and goal oriented. My mother explained it further to me: "You all were learning academics at the same time, and I tried my best to stick to the schedule while balancing free time."

She went on to talk about the day being like a regular school day: "I tried duplicating what we know as a regular school day when it came to different subject periods and times for you all to eat and socialize." She said our school day was from 9:00 a.m. until about 1:00 p.m. I still have flashbacks of doing work in the phonics book my mother taught from. Learning the basics of literacy under my mother's guidance was crucial for my early childhood success.

Another benefit of being home-schooled was the food. I mean, let's be honest: With a limited number of choices, school lunches are not always the best. Snack and lunch times were gratifying. Each stage of life has its pros and cons and home-schooling certainly provided both for my family.

One of the challenges of being home-schooled was the limited amount of personal space that we had to move around and learn. We did have three rooms on the first floor of our home, but they were not very spacious. We were all taught on just one table in the dining room, each of us working on appropriate grade-level materials. Furthermore, our social contacts throughout the school day were exclusively with our family members.

These challenges did not compare to the overwhelming benefits from our educational experience. Looking back on all the awards and achievements we have obtained in school and in life, I can objectively say that my mother was an amazing educator and had a positive impact on the education of her six children. And although my mother was our main teacher, she did have a great teaching assistant, my father, who also taught us valuable life lessons.

Overall, it was hard for all eight of us to live together. We dealt with many heartaches, pain, laughter, and fun, but at the end of the day, we were close-knit and loved each other unconditionally. The bond we had led to many happy times but some hectic moments as well.

Living together as kids, teenagers, and all the way into our twenties, led to some interesting and unique circumstances. When we were younger and as we got older, space was limited and watching our favorite TV shows and movies proved difficult as the television was the hot commodity. We always wanted to watch TV at the same time. When we lived in Queens, we had only one TV. My parents had to create schedules and times when each of us were allowed to watch TV.

The lack of privacy was another contentious issue. When we lived together, we had to share rooms. This created uncomfortable situations because there was rarely a time when one of us was alone in a room for more than five minutes. That was simply the reality growing up with eight people living in one home. We could not watch a TV show alone, eat alone, or play alone. Of course, many things are more fun to do with others, but sometimes it is nice to have a little personal space. Personal space for us was nowhere to be found.

Being young, immature, and living with seven other people was extremely hard for me growing up. I would not say that I was the worst kid ever, but I did not always act appropriately. Although I regret and have since apologized for all the wrong and hurtful things I did to my siblings, I still feel bad and somewhat guilty to this day. From playing around at times, to serious fights, things got out of hand a few too many times. My parents did an excellent job of combating my negative behaviors and outbursts as a teenager, but sometimes when they were not home, things got ugly.

There were fights that lasted a few minutes, and unfortunately, there were fights that lasted several hours. I remember one time I was being so defiant when my parents were not home, and I started arguing about the smallest issue. Next thing you know, I was on the ground being restrained by Lauren, Christy, and David. I was refusing to cooperate and was bothering everyone in the house.

My siblings were holding me down like I was an untamed animal. All I remember was being held down on the ground and Lauren screaming, "Daniel, you better stop!" Then, yelling to Maria Grace a few minutes later due to my continued defiance: "Call the police!" Eventually I listened and was able to calm down in my room before the police were called.

The worst fight I recall was when I had just started college. David and I were home alone. We each had a friend over, and I do not even know how it started, but one thing led to another, and we got into a fight that lasted for several hours, with my friend and his friend continuously trying to break us up. We were getting on each other's nerves, trading back and forth petty, annoying comments that perpetuated the quarrel.

I felt bad because as the older brother I should have swallowed my pride and just ignored him, regardless of who was right or wrong. I ended up hitting David in the face and leaving the house to stay at my friend's house for the rest of the night. Mark was furious, heard about what happened, and ended up driving out to Mount Sinai all the way from Queens (where he was living) to stay the night in case anything else happened between us.

That fight was my biggest regret because David and I went an entire year after the fight without speaking to each other. Thankfully, a few years after the fight, our relationship was repaired. The blood, sweat, and tears that we experienced were unnecessary and unfortunate. That altercation and a few others thankfully did not turn deadly, although some of them were quite dangerous.

Here was another dangerous altercation: One afternoon, my Uncle Joey got a phone call from one of his close friends, who happened to live right across the street from our house. My uncle picked up the phone, said hello to his friend Marty, then Marty quickly replied: "Joey, hey, it's Marty. Listen, I don't know who it is, but Mark is hanging either Daniel or David out of the third-floor window. You better get over here right away...." Again, we were happy that none of our altercations turned deadly.

Although there were challenges that came alongside living with a big family in one home, there were definitely many more positive aspects. Six kids and two adults certainly created messes in the house, but six kids also made it easier and faster to clean the messes we made. Doing things like decorating the Christmas tree together or cleaning the house made each process more efficient. We showed effective teamwork working together more times than not. My parents had us clean daily and rightfully so. Although we complained, cleaning was not hard at all, especially when we worked as a team.

Playing board games and other games were fun and intense, to say the least. Games like Red Light, Green Light, Monopoly, Pick-up Sticks, and Candy Land were our favorite games. My family and I also played sports all the time when we were younger. While my sisters were in the porch trying to see who could walk and stay on the balance beam the longest, my two brothers and I could be found outside playing basketball or another sport we aggressively competed at.

Playing these sports together as a family was a positive aspect of having a big family because we played frequently and made each other better. The older siblings usually prevailed in any game played, but the younger ones learned from them and improved their skills, and occasionally, pulled off the unthinkable upset. David and I were not better than Mark at basketball, but here and there we pulled out the win. I figured if David could beat Goliath, we could beat our older brother in a meaningless basketball game once in a while. Maria Grace felt the same way about her two older sisters as they competed in the porch on the balance beam doing gymnastics.

Through the guidance and teaching of our parents and the willingness to forgive, even if it took days, months, or even a year, the love we had proved to be priceless. There were times it took blood, sweat, and tears to feel the love we had, but in the end, the love was always present. We all knew then and know now that love is kind, and when at times we were not so kind to each other, we felt it inside, and it hurt. Then, we stepped up to the plate and forgave each other when we needed to. That is how love is and that is how love will always be: forgiving and unending.

When I think about all our past experiences, I know we learned from our mistakes because of the success we have obtained. And when I reflect on every memorable moment, I know in the end there was love, like described in the Bible: "Love is patient, love is kind. It does not envy, it does not boast, it is not proud. It is not rude, it is not self-seeking, it is not easily angered; it keeps no record of wrongs. Love does not delight in evil but rejoices with the truth. It always protects, always trusts, always hopes, and always perseveres. Love never fails."

Trying to do these things daily to become a loving person is understandably difficult, but with hard work and teamwork, it can be accomplished. With the help of my family (my teammates), I became a loving person. Love is a process and a choice, so be patient and choose love because it is unwavering and unbelievable.

An Inspirational Quote for You

"Nothing is perfect in this world. Everything has its pros and cons."

—Nivendita Sharma

Like I mentioned throughout this chapter, pros and cons are inevitable in each aspect of life, but if you stay positive, the cons can be overcome and may eventually turn into pros. You must adapt to every situation and change that you encounter with patience, kindness, and love, especially at home with your family. There is always going to be good and bad, convenient and inconvenient in life, so try to find the beauty in everything.

THREE

The Struggle

I was nine years old when my mother stopped home-schooling me. It was now time to take what I had learned and use it in a classroom setting. My mother taught me how to read and write, and how to problem solve, which are vital factors in the elementary and middle school years. She laid down the foundation, and now it was time to take those skills and apply them in school with teachers who for once would not be named Mrs. Casamassa. This was one of the most difficult trials I faced growing up.

I started attending school officially in third grade at St. John's Lutheran School. This school was located about ten minutes away from our home in Queens. It was a small school that serviced students in kindergarten through eighth grade. It was a unique school because of the age disparity between the youngest students, who were five years old, compared to the oldest students, who were 14 years old. My third grade teacher was Ms. H. She was a wonderful teacher who helped me make the transition from home-school to the classroom.

Since it was a Lutheran school, we had daily chapel activities where students received spiritual comfort and knowledge about the "good word." Everyone in the school had to wear a required outfit; girls wore skirts, and the boys wore dress pants with a shirt and tie. The class sizes were what we know to be normal for a classroom setting, approximately 25 students in each class. I loved all the specials like gym, music, etc., but it was the academics that I did not like.

Academically in third grade, I started to show signs of deficiency in my subject areas. Although it was similar to what my mother taught during home-school, the subjects seemed harder and more difficult to complete. Ms. H., along with my mother helping me after school, were the reasons I was able to get through the difficult times and academic struggles during my first year in school.

After completing third grade, I moved on to fourth grade at St. John's Lutheran School. My teacher was Ms. M. She was also a good teacher who tried her best to help me succeed. In fourth grade I started having mixed feelings about school, and academically, I was becoming noticeably frustrated.

Fourth grade was the first year I started receiving more academic assistance outside of school. In fact, late in fourth grade, I was examined by the New York City Committee for Special Education. I was classified as "learning disabled with a language delay." Because of the lack of educational services at St. John's, I went to another school to receive extra help after school.

I remember my Aunt Joanie picking me up early from St. John's a few times a week to attend another school for extra services to help improve my learning disability and speech impairment. My parents thought of holding me back a grade level because of my difficulties in class along with a poor score I received on a standardized test, but in the end, they did not make that decision.

In fifth grade, I had Ms. C. as a teacher. She was one of my favorite teachers because she always made the learning fun. Even though she helped me out and was a great teacher, I still had difficulty learning and controlling my emotions. During this school year, I started acting out and exhibiting challenging behaviors.

I remember vividly many of the poor decisions I made that year, especially this one: One of my classmates got up from her seat to speak with the teacher. I then quickly and secretly walked behind her chair. The conversation with her and Ms. C. had ended, so she started walking back to her seat. As she sat down, I quickly pulled the chair out from under her, and she loudly and embarrassingly hit the classroom floor. She began crying, and I felt so bad. That decision got me in so much trouble, and I had to face severe consequences.

I also recall starting a food fight in the lunchroom with a few of my classmates in fifth grade. This became a big mess in and out of the lunchroom, as I paid the price for my actions again. During these three years at St. John's, my mother was a kindergarten teacher in the school. I remember a few times when they had to call her up to my classroom to speak with me about my behavior. My mother let me have it during school, while at the same time, trying to be calm and professional. When I got home from school, she reprimanded me again and punished me for my actions.

After these three years, I was psychologically evaluated. My emotional issues seemed the most concerning at the time. I would frequently shut down in school and have these quiet moments where I would not communicate or talk to anyone. My parents were becoming concerned that I was falling into depression, something they hoped was not true. The psychological evaluations along with the Wechsler Individual Achievement Test (W.I.A.T.) were administered to see how I was doing both psychologically and academically.

The tests and evidence from my classroom behaviors showed that I had anger problems, signs of depression, and significant deficiencies in the areas of writing and reading comprehension. Furthermore, the tests showed specifically that I had "processing difficulties" in speech and language. I was eligible for extra assistance, which I received more extensively in sixth grade. After being able to get by academically, emotionally, and behaviorally in a school setting for three years without any major problems, it was now time for a change.

I started sixth grade at P.S. 66, a Queens public school. St. John's Lutheran certainly had its temptations, but this school it seemed, at age 11, had many more. One of the reasons was due to the fact that there were simply more students in the school. The other reason was that I was now attending a public school, as opposed to St. John's, a private school, which seemed to have stricter standards for behavior.

Moreover, at this time with my already crammed educational background, I knew I needed to start trying harder in class. Along with trying harder, I needed to begin controlling my emotions and not shut down as often as I did the previous three years. I received a lot of educational support. While I was receiving help in school, my parents hired a private tutor to provide additional support outside of school. The tutor and I got along well. She helped reinforce things I was learning in school and taught me other skills as well.

In the summer of sixth grade, my parents were trying to decide what school would be the best option to assist my troubles and help me succeed both academically and behaviorally. P.S. 66 only went up to sixth grade, and they had to choose a school by the end of the summer. St. John's Lutheran School was still an option, but they did not think it was a good idea for me to go back there again. They contemplated it for a few weeks, going over all the possible options and then made a decision. After doing some research, they found a school they thought could help me succeed.

Louis Armstrong Middle School (LAMS) was their final choice. This school is located in Flushing Queens and serves over a thousand students in grades 5-8. Louis Armstrong Middle School had many accommodations and modifications for students with disabilities. The staff at the school made it a priority to mix the general population with the "students with special needs" throughout the day. With the school's rich background in music, hence the school's name, fine arts classes were a popular choice for most students.

The school was named after Louis Armstrong, who was one of the most influential jazz artists of all-time and lived a complex and inspired life. That alone gave me some hope and inspiration. At age 12, I was now inching closer toward my teenage years and attending another school. When my parents made the decision to send me to LAMS, I was sad and upset. I gave my mother a hard time because I did not want to attend another school all by myself. My mother, trying to ease the pain, made another decision.

My mother asked my sister Christy to attend the school with me on a temporary basis. My mother wanted the initial experience to be less stressful, so I could concentrate on my academics and focus on improving my present emotional state. Christy unselfishly agreed. My sister, just a year younger than me, started in sixth grade. We saw each other daily and that alone made my day and helped to relieve my nervous feelings. Eventually, when I got more acclimated to the school, Christy went back to the school she was previously attending, P.S. 210.

Due to the evaluations I received that school year (1996-1997) and some prior years, along with other valuable material, I continued to receive related services within the general education setting at LAMS. Whether it was extra time allotted on tests, or directions being read to me, I was receiving extensive help and was trying to get through the last two years of middle school without any major issues occurring.

I was finally entering the last month of seventh grade. The year took forever. My mother and father worked hard trying to set me up with the right tools and resources that were needed to get through that transitional year, which was filled with many additional academic challenges. One way my parents did that was by getting me another tutor outside of school to keep me focused on my schoolwork.

My parents were not only busy with their jobs, but with taking care of my siblings as well. This meant that I had to start becoming more independent and willing to accept the help of others. I did not like doing homework, but the tutor was motivating me to complete it daily. I thrived during those tutoring sessions and the smaller school setting at LAMS.

My last year at LAMS had its ups and downs. Although the year passed without any major issues, I was still struggling academically and behaviorally, and my parents were very concerned. Now that middle school had officially ended, they were wondering where I should attend high school. Before that question was answered, there was one big question my parents had to answer first: Where would our new home be?

An Inspirational Quote for You

"Our greatest weakness lies in giving up. The most certain way to succeed is always to try just one more time."

– Thomas Edison

Thomas Edison created the first lightbulb, but it was not created right away. He tried many times and went through years of struggle. In fact, he worked on over three thousand theories before he came up with an efficient lightbulb. Thomas Edison could easily have given up, but he stayed strong and persevered until he found success.

There are always going to be things in life that make us want to give up, but if we fight through them, we can look back and feel more confident the next time a trial in life arrives. For many people today, school is difficult to face. It was always challenging for me, but I continued to press on because I believed that I would eventually succeed, just like Thomas Edison.

FOUR

Against All Odds

The high school years are usually the most challenging for students. They certainly were for me. Before starting high school, my family and I moved to Mount Sinai on Long Island after my mother accepted a teaching job in the Sachem Central School District.

Our new home did not have as many floors as our Queens house, so my brother David and I shared a room at first, and my three sisters shared a room as well. Mark got the prestigious honor of having his own bedroom, although I did not care about that. All I worried about at the time was what high school would be like. I was anxious and already feeling the effects of the move to Long Island. I knew that high school was going to be a challenging transition.

I officially started high school in September of 1999. I had to find new friends and meet new teachers. I was frightened and nervous when I started ninth grade and just walking in the hallways made me nervous. I was so small and skinny, and all the other guys, especially those on the football team, were muscular and big. I was happy that my sister Lauren was there to support me, as she was a junior at the time.

In the fall of ninth grade, I made the J.V. basketball team at Mount Sinai, which helped ease the stress and nervousness I felt as a new student in a new town. I did not end up playing much during that season because there were other players that were simply better, stronger, and more skilled. Overall, it was still an accomplishment that made a difference early in my high school career.

I was feeling good athletically, but behaviorally I was not doing well. I started becoming more comfortable in school and was no longer shy, especially when it came to seeking attention. I made a few friends that year, who turned out to be negative influences in my life. I was very disruptive in my classes and acted extremely immature.

Academically, things were very difficult because I was struggling to read and comprehend grade-level texts. I remember being given these tough assignments in English class where we had to read a passage and then answer questions. The passages seemed so long and the words too difficult to understand. I became frustrated because I could not do the work, so I started acting out in class. I felt helpless and all alone.

My parents became concerned about me both academically and behaviorally, more than they did during my elementary and middle school years. The staff and administration became concerned, too, so they set up a meeting to discuss my behavioral and academic needs. On December 7, 1999, the Committee on Special Education met to review my educational background and to decide on an appropriate placement for me. The committee sent a letter home to my mother regarding their decision a few weeks later:

> Dear Mrs. Maria Casamassa:
> On behalf of the Board of Education, I am writing to inform you of the Committee on Special Education's determination regarding special education services for your child, Daniel Casamassa. Below, you will see the recommendations developed by the Committee on Special Education on 12/07/1999 and reviewed by the Board of Education on 12/21/1999.
> Current Placement: Resource Room
> Classification: Learning Disabled

My parents knew it was not because of them that I was being placed in a special education setting, but they could not help but feel partially responsible. They did not fail, I did. They did the best they could; I just never met them halfway as I should have.

This placement seemed good initially, but my stubbornness and learning difficulties made the placement a challenging one. One of the positive aspects of this placement, though, was that I received accommodations and modifications that helped me to concentrate and focus more on schoolwork and tests. I received extra time to take tests, a separate location to take tests, and also had my special education teachers reading the tests to me. These modifications and accommodations assisted me greatly, but unfortunately, it still was not enough.

Even with the tests being read to me, I still found it very difficult to understand the questions and answer them correctly. I was always looking for my teachers to suggest or imply which were the correct answers, but they never did.

After being classified with a learning disability, I was taken out of class more often for related services and was not around my friends much anymore. My special education classes were located at the end of a long hallway. Other students in the school noticed I was attending these classes, which made me feel embarrassed and ashamed. I remember being called a "Sped" in school countless times. They were referring to the words "special" and "education" and using it negatively to describe my status as a student with a disability.

I started feeling angry and sad inside. I was ashamed and it made me resist the help even more. I always remember speed walking to my special education classes so none of my peers saw me in the hallway. That alone led me to reject the efforts of my teachers and dislike my placement. I did not feel "cool" as a special education student, and at the time, I thought high school was all about fitting in and being cool.

All of these diagnoses and placements were making me crazy; I did not know what to do. I was not getting good grades, and I was doing more fooling around than learning when I went to Resource Room. All of my teachers and classmates were noticing me more, but for all the wrong reasons. I received detention and in-school suspension regularly, and I would make many immature decisions just to get people to accept me as their "friend."

I remember having to serve in-school suspension one time because of my poor decision in the cafeteria during lunch. This is what happened: I was hanging out with my friends in the back of the cafeteria waiting for the bell to ring. I decided to take a full Gatorade bottle and launch it all the way toward the front of the cafeteria. The next noise heard was a loud bang! The bottle punctured a huge hole in the awning above the cooking area. The entire cafeteria went quiet for five seconds. Everyone looked around and a few teachers started looking to find the student who threw the bottle. As the teachers on lunch duty started looking around, of course they walked toward me, and I knew I was in big trouble.

Supposedly, one of the teachers who had lunch duty was positive that I was the culprit, and he pulled me out of the cafeteria and walked me down to the office. I denied throwing the bottle to him, so we waited to meet with the principal. This teacher was furious and kept trying to get me to admit what I had done, but I continued to lie and deny my wrongdoing.

Five minutes later, still waiting in the office with the teacher, he had me write down my name on a piece of paper. Now I am thinking: *What is going on and why do I have to write down my name?* After writing down my name, he then asked me to write down my name again, this time with my right hand (I am a lefty). After struggling to write down my name with my right hand, he took the pencil and paper from me and said, "Yep, you are a lefty. I know that you tossed that bottle because I saw a left hand in the air when the bottle was thrown. Nice try!"

That encounter in the office and others that year reassured me of one thing: There were many people much smarter than me. I finally admitted to throwing the bottle and served the in-school suspension the following three days.

June finally arrived, and I had finished up ninth grade. I was able to complete that school year without any other major episodes in school, but I was becoming increasingly moody and frustrated. Finally, the summer was here, and I was relieved and excited to have some freedom. Because of the poor grades that I received in ninth grade, I had to attend summer school that year or else I would be in danger of getting left back. I was able to get through my summer school classes without any academic setbacks.

Ninth grade was finally over, and I was preparing to start 10th grade at Mount Sinai High School. The Board of Education had to make their annual decision based on the Subcommittee on Special Education and their determination regarding my placement. The recommendation that was developed and reviewed by the Board of Education for 10th grade was "mainstreaming," also known as inclusion in the regular education setting. I also had to continue attending classes in Resource Room. My parents informed me of this decision and gave me some words of encouragement before the school year started.

10th Grade

The first few months of the 2000-2001 school year did not go well. The only thing that encouraged me as I began 10th grade was that I had made the basketball team again. My social studies class in particular, was a disaster. I had a good regular education teacher and special education teacher, but I refused to learn, and it was also hard to pay attention.

It was difficult to concentrate during this class and other classes because I had Attention-Deficit/Hyperactivity Disorder (ADHD). When it was time to read in class, I struggled mightily. Because I was significantly below grade level in reading, most of the words on the pages were too difficult to decode and comprehend. On top of this, my ADHD made the reading process more difficult because of my hyperactivity and my inability to pay attention for long periods of time. The combination of a learning disability and a mental health disorder was making school much more challenging for me. Most days in school I would just sit there quietly, feeling depressed. I was beginning each day tired and stressed out. My parents were noticeably concerned, seeing my mood swings and personality change in the blink of an eye at home. I was acting out one day and quiet the next day.

After getting through the first few months of the school year, the Subcommittee on Special Education conducted another meeting on December 20, 2000. Based on test results and reports, they recommended continuing the in-school counseling sessions, but most significantly, the committee recommended a psychiatric evaluation. The school psychologist and Director of Pupil Personnel Services at school referred me for a psychiatric evaluation.

The psychologist wrote up a summary of the behaviors I was exhibiting in and out of school. She mentioned how I was becoming "increasingly distractible" in class. She went on to write that I had been "resistant to any school-based therapy." These statements by my school's psychologist were troubling for my parents and the Committee on Special Education (CSE).

The CSE wanted to "investigate" the possibility that I was "depressed." They also wanted to examine the possibility of substance abuse. Additionally, the CSE wanted to determine whether my school placement was an appropriate one.

My father accompanied me to the psychiatric evaluation on January 24, 2001, five days after I turned 16. I was in the room when the psychiatrist began interviewing him. My father stated that he noticed I was becoming more "physically and verbally abusive" over the past few years at home. He went on to discuss specifics, indicating that I "become easily frustrated" when asked to do something around the house.

My father also disclosed the fact that I once "took the family car without permission." When I heard my father telling the psychiatrist all of this, I was embarrassed and ashamed. The psychiatrist went on to talk about a Person in Need of Supervision (PINS) petition. She did not think I would be eligible for that program because of my age, but it was brought up as a possibility. Nonetheless, after these discussions, the psychiatrist recommended a few things for my school and parents to consider.

The psychiatrist first recommended that I be considered for a "therapeutically-oriented academic program with a high teacher-to-student ratio." Next, she suggested that I be given antidepressants to control and regulate my "discouraged state." That was something my parents did not want me experimenting with because they adhered to a more holistic approach to health.

The psychiatrist went on to discuss again the possibility of being eligible for a PINS management program. Moreover, she talked about my success in the workplace and therefore recommended looking into a vocational program that she thought would be "helpful."

Lastly, in the psychiatrist's report, she added in her "Diagnostic Impression." A Diagnostic Impression is considered a doctor's initial opinion. Below you will see all the different types of disorders that the psychiatrist listed in her report, along with her assessment of my current IQ, which was "Borderline intellectual functioning" at the time.

DIAGNOSTIC IMPRESSION:	
Axis I:	Dysthymic Disorder
	Oppositional Defiant Disorder
	R/O Attention Deficit Hyperactivity Disorder
	R/O Substance abuse
Axis II:	Reading Disorder
	Disorder of Written Expression
	Mixed Receptive and Expressive Communication Disorder
	Borderline intellectual functioning
Axis III:	Environmental allergies
	H/O lead poisoning
Axis IV:	Code 2 - Mild psychosocial stressors
Axis V:	Current GAF: 40
	Highest GAF in the past year: 40

My parents took a few of her recommendations seriously, and the one that took effect first was the recommendation they were reluctant to pursue. After discussions with the school, my parents decided to put me on antidepressants. They brought me to another psychiatrist a few weeks later in February of 2001. I was officially treated for Major Depressive Disorder.

A few weeks later, the same doctor recommended that I be home tutored until the medication dosage was adjusted. My parents agreed with the recommendation and felt it would be beneficial since I was not succeeding in school. I started getting home tutored in March of 2001. Before home tutoring began, the CSE met one more time to review the psychiatrist's findings and the doctor's recommendation.

The most significant issue discussed was whether to amend my "Learning Disabled" classification and change it to an "Emotional Disturbance" classification. The consideration was later rejected, and my "Learning Disabled" classification remained in place. They also discussed developing a Behavior Intervention Plan (BIP) to address my behavioral needs. Overall, the meeting focused on my new placement: home tutoring.

I was relieved to receive home tutoring for the remainder of the school year. The school had too many distractions, and I was not able to focus academically. I was also being negatively influenced by my "friends" and peers to make bad decisions. Looking back now, I am happy that my parents and the CSE made the decision to take me out of school.

During the home-schooling sessions, learning and concentrating was easier, something I never experienced in the school setting. My learning difficulties and behavior problems were so serious that I vividly remember my father writing me countless letters expressing his concerns. Most importantly, though, the letters were filled with words of encouragement. My father was trying to do all he could through his letters to encourage me so that I would not give up.

Moreover, during this year and the prior two years, I was stealing money from my siblings and parents on a regular basis. Along with this bad habit and others, I knew deep down that I needed to make a change quickly before something worse happened in my life.

After a few months of being home tutored, my 10th grade year filled with turmoil and hardship was finally over. Because of my poor grades, I had to attend summer school once again. Fortunately, I was able to get through summer school without any significant setbacks. Also, during this summer, the CSE decided that it would be best for me to repeat 10th grade. Although it was the right decision, it made me feel worse inside. My parents were disappointed but continued to stay faithful that a turnaround would eventually happen.

10th Grade...Again

After getting through the first few months of the 2001-2002 school year, the CSE, along with the approval of my parents, made a tough but appropriate decision. A change of scenery was needed. November 18, 2001, was my final day attending Mount Sinai. I said bye to the few friends I had and then just like that, I was gone. Nesaquake Learning Center was my new school as of November 19, 2001. This learning center was part of Eastern Suffolk BOCES at the time and served students on Long Island who had disabilities. A mini school bus picked me up every morning along with other students who lived in neighboring towns. The bus ride to school was long, but I always slept to diminish the emotional pain, at least temporarily.

The first few weeks at my new school went well and because of the small classes, I made new friends quickly. I also liked the teachers I had. As January 2002 approached, something clicked inside of me as I started to mature. This new chapter in my life was the wake-up call I desperately needed.

Everything at Nesaquake Learning Center seemed less stressful. The school also had less distractions and several staff members helping to educate me. I began my time there quietly and still shell-shocked. Eventually, I became accustomed to my new school and flourished during the first few months there. I felt less pressure to perform academically than I did at Mount Sinai.

When you become a teenager, it is hard to say no to peer pressure and temptations. Mount Sinai did try very hard to support me and keep me away from temptations, but I always seemed to say yes to peer pressure when I simply needed to say no. The temptations to make bad decisions subsided drastically from day one at Nesaquake. The first reason being the fact that there were simply more staff members supervising the students, and secondly because of my willingness to try harder, one thing I greatly regret not doing at Mount Sinai.

Also, the workload at Nesaquake seemed less intense, and I was also given work that was geared toward my reading and writing levels. The teachers differentiated the work for me, and I also never felt rushed to complete assignments, since students were given extra periods to complete work throughout the week. Most importantly, the teachers at Nesaquake gave rewards and free time to students who behaved and did all their work by the end of the week. These rewards helped me succeed.

There was also no more time for games at Nesaquake. This was my last chance. Getting transferred to another school because of my behavioral and academic failures was a tough pill for me to swallow, so I had to change quickly. My family and others were praying for me nonstop, and my teachers and counselors were collaborating tirelessly to make this transition work. All involved knew the task was a difficult one after hearing about my troubled past as a student in Queens and at Mount Sinai High School.

For the most part, I stayed away from the negative influences during my time at Nesaquake. At that point in life, I had stressed out my parents and past teachers to the fullest, and I was starting to feel sorry for what I had put them through. I was determined to make better decisions.

At Mount Sinai, each class had approximately 25 students, but at Nesaquake, there were only six to eight students in each class and approximately 100 students in the entire building. For me, that was crucial to my academic success. Because of this, I flourished academically and socially. I did not succeed in a large classroom environment, so the choice to send me to BOCES was a life-changing decision.

My second attempt at completing 10th grade was successful. I finally felt confident academically. The work felt easier, and the individualized focus of the staff helped immensely. Things were starting to improve academically, but out of school, my negative behaviors continued.

All of my friends from BOCES did not live in my town or even near my town, so I was still hanging out with the wrong crowd from Mount Sinai. My parents started growing overly concerned. I was sneaking out of my house in the middle of the night to meet up with my friends. We would drive by random mailboxes and knock them down. I was too irresponsible at the time to realize that those actions were disrespectful and unlawful. I remember one time sneaking out and not being able to make it home to sleep in my own bed.

This is what happened: My father was watching TV in the living room. With a plan already in mind, I quickly jumped over the banister of the stairs to avoid him and headed toward the kitchen. I crawled onto the floor through the kitchen and silently entered the garage. I collided into a few random things on the floor in the garage and luckily did not make too much noise. While trying to find my way in the pitch dark, I opened the garage door and ran outside and down the block where my friends were waiting to pick me up.

I was so excited about hanging out with my friends that I never thought about the repercussions of getting caught. After a night of "fun" with my friends, I got dropped off down the block from my house. It was now 1:00 a.m. I ran back to my house as quietly as possible. I proceeded to the back door that

I wisely left unlocked. But as I went to open the door, it was locked. Then, a flashlight shined on my face. I jumped back, frightened! I saw my father's angry face. At first, he did not see me.

He called out, "Who is there?"

I conceded right away, "It is me, Daniel!"

My father heard my voice, shut the door, and did not allow me back in the house. He wanted me to learn a lesson. Approximately five minutes later, I saw headlights shining outside of my house. I wondered where the lights were coming from, so I walked out front to inquire. It was the cops! (I must have made too much noise trying to sneak back into the house, so my father not knowing it was me, called the cops before he had seen me for fear that someone was trying to break in.) My father and the cop approached me, which caught me off guard. The cop asked me a few questions about where I was the entire night.

After a few minutes of intense questioning, the cop asked my father the most important question:

"Do you want me to take him in?"

"Yes, take him in," my father replied.

After that quick conversation, I was handcuffed and taken to jail. The next day I was released and allowed to finally go home. My father did not make that decision because he thought I committed some heinous crime. He did it because he wanted me to learn a lesson. For me it was a lesson learned because staying overnight in a jail cell was terrifying as a young, lost teenager. I was not a criminal, but I certainly was not acting like a sane member of society either.

My parents were pleased with the academic progress I was showing in school, but they were still worried and upset about my behavior at home and in the neighborhood. They got so desperate and had no other choice, so they sent me away. The trip only lasted one day, but my parents wanted me to wake up, similar to the wake-up call I got in school that year. My parents sent me to "Hope House Ministries" in Port Jefferson, 10 minutes from our home.

Hope House Ministries provides "hope" to young male teenagers in need of housing, restoration, and lifestyle change. The basis of their program is to provide competent residential and counseling assistance to those in need and families dealing with a "crisis." For my parents, I was the "crisis." Socially and behaviorally, this was just what I needed.

I was brought there by my father to stay the night and see how it went and if I liked the program. The experience went well. I was able to meet other struggling teenagers, some dealing with serious addictions and others who were homeless. We talked and ate together and even played some basketball. I did enjoy my time there and understood that my father was trying to help, but I did not want to live there for the foreseeable future.

My father picked me up the next morning and drove me to school. He asked me how it went and if I liked the place and people. I did not say much, but my father understood by the tone of my voice that I did not want to live there. It might have ended up being a life-changing event, but I did not want to move away from my family. I loved them so much, even though I did not show it most of the time. This overnight stay at Hope House did wake me up because I started to realize how precious life and my family truly were.

During my second year repeating 10th grade, my parents tried their best to get me to know the Lord more, so I could turn my life around. They decided to bring me to church every Sunday morning, but I was always in a bad mood when we were on the way to church. I would usually just sleep on the half-hour ride to church and would not say much on the way home. My parents would ask a few questions on the way home, with one question always being, "How did you like the service?" I always told them the service was "good" even though that was far from reality.

I would sit in the balcony, and my parents would sit downstairs, right in the front of the sanctuary. Midway through the church service, I remember many times just walking out because I was bored. I would just wander around the church looking for things to do and people to see.

Unfortunately, I did not want anything to do with the actual church service. Looking back now, I am sad that I made those decisions to leave the service and reject the gospel. Thankfully, I kept on attending church with my parents every Sunday.

My second attempt to successfully complete 10th grade had finally ended. Academically, I was flourishing in school, and behaviorally, I obviously still had a lot to learn...two polar opposites. I now had to look deeper and search wider to resolve my issues. Fortunately, my parents were always there for me as I looked deeper and searched wider.

11th Grade

After taking two years to complete 10th grade, it was finally time for 11th grade (2002-2003 school year). Because I did so well at Nesaquake Learning Center, all who were involved with my educational placement agreed it was best that I stay in BOCES for another school year. I was happy with that decision.

Although it was the same program, it was no longer located in St. James. The school moved to Bellport, which is located on the south shore of Long Island. It was renamed Bellport Academic Center. Although it was the same program, the new name and location gave it a new meaning. One of the best aspects of my new school was that I was able to study a trade, which was funded by Mount Sinai School District. I was able to study a trade at the Brookhaven Technical Center, which was a separate school but attached to the Bellport Academic Center.

As the school year started, I got more acclimated to the new school system, and I was thriving as a student. The first three hours of the day consisted of attending the technical school to study a trade, which was TV Production. I did not think I had a future in that field, but it was still a great experience and kept me out of trouble.

I was able to use real cameras to shoot live shows, which we did in the studio. As a class, we were then able to edit parts of replica shows that we portrayed. We learned how to be newscasters, weathermen, etc. I had so much fun during the first part of my school day and did not want to leave, but I had to continue improving academically in my subject areas. My tech. class started at 7:45 a.m., so when I arrived at Bellport Academic Center later in the morning, there was still more than half the day left for me to learn.

Mr. Aikin, my homeroom teacher, was the greatest influence on my life in high school. He taught me how to be patient in tough times, and he also taught me how to become a great writer. His teaching assistant was Ms. Friscina. She was my school mother, always advising me not to get caught up in any drama that was unhealthy or that interfered with my education.

I also remember the days when I was able to play basketball with the gym coaches. I would be on my best behavior and finish my work quickly to earn some free time. Playing basketball always helped to relieve the stress and depression that I felt at times.

The rest of my junior year at BOCES went smoothly; I was maturing nicely in school, and surprisingly, out of school, too. I began to attend church more frequently. Also, I started owning up to my wrongdoings, instead of denying them. No longer was I taking drugs for major depressive disorder. I was beginning to see things more clearly. I was not an angel out of school, but I was certainly improving compared to the past few years of high school.

I was re-evaluated in May of 2003, the end of my junior year, which produced mixed results. The psychologist at school performed the evaluation and then stated the following: "Daniel works independently within the classroom and completes class and home assignments. He is described as an attentive, compliant student, and his on-task performance is adequate."

Although the psychologist had positive comments to describe my work ethic, she also noted in her report that I still had "significant academic difficulties." During that school year, I achieved a grade equivalent of 4.1 in math and 3.2 in reading on the "Stanford" assessment. Even with the mixed results, my parents were still happy that I was working harder in school. Even though I was in 11th grade reading on a third-grade level and performing on a fourth-grade level in math, I knew those scores were based on many years of struggle, which could not be fixed overnight.

My successful junior year had ended; I had a good feeling about my senior year. For the first time as a high school student, I was looking forward to my summer, finally without having to attend summer school. That summer I stayed out of trouble and stayed home most of the time, so I would not be tempted to fall back into bad habits.

12th Grade

In the 2003-2004 school year, Christy and I were both seniors in high school because of the fact that I had gotten left back. That was a unique experience, to say the least. I couldn't change the past, and it did not bother me that I was in the same grade as Christy. I was finally a senior and starting another year at Bellport Academic Center. Although I liked the school, I wanted to prove that I could succeed in a regular education setting for the first time in my life.

The first few months of the 2003-2004 school year at BOCES were spectacular. I was now studying plumbing and heating in my tech. school, and I was maintaining good grades. The finish line was in the near future, and I wanted to pass through it with full force. The plan was to finish off at BOCES in January, play on Mount Sinai's varsity basketball team, then graduate alongside Christy and our classmates back at Mount Sinai.

From September to December of 2003, I worked diligently to reach my goal. After completing all my academic requirements during those months and looking like a role model and remade man, it was time to make the transition my parents, BOCES, and myself were all eagerly waiting for.

I was ready to succeed and prove to all the doubters that I could indeed control my emotions and perform at a high level back at Mount Sinai. I wanted to go "home" where I belonged. I also wanted a chance to apply my improved basketball skills and prove that I was no fluke on the court.

It was now January 2004, a few weeks before my 19th birthday, and once again I was walking the halls of Mount Sinai High School. Most importantly, during that school year on April 27, I was re-evaluated late in the year by the Committee on Special Education. As a result of all my academic success at BOCES, they declassified my "Learning Disabled" status, which officially took effect once the school year ended. That was a joy to hear and something that seemed far-fetched just a few short years earlier.

Being able to redeem myself and play basketball again in my home district also made me feel good. The basketball season was a blessing from above. But before playing, I had to attend a hearing with my basketball coach, the Athletic Director, and a few high-ranking officials representing Long Island sports to regain eligibility again to play basketball. I was thankful during the meeting, and I spoke about my intentions and willingness to "work hard" and not waste this opportunity. After the meeting, I found out that I was deemed eligible to play as a fifth-year senior.

The season went well and although I did not play as much as I would have liked, I was grateful when I did. I had not played basketball for Mount Sinai in a few years, and I understood that there were other players more deserving of playing time because of the simple fact that they had been playing together at Mount Sinai for their entire high school career, and even since middle school.

Nonetheless, I worked hard during practice and showed my coach how much I improved. I was hustling all over the court during practices, scoring baskets on the starters, and even defending them on defense. The hard work in practice finally paid off as the coach called my number during a few important games that our team needed to win.

My coach, rightly so, was reluctant at times to put me in because of my history of anger issues and behavioral problems. I will never forget one game, though, we lost, and my coach came up to me after the game and said the following: "Hey, Dan, I am sorry I never put you into the game. We could have used you out there tonight to bring up the ball and break the press...." I replied, "It is okay, Coach, I will be ready whenever you need me."

I was disappointed that I did not play in that game or as much as I wanted to that season, but I was grateful to at least be part of an organized team, something I could not handle or do early on in my high school career. There is one person, though, that made that basketball season for me a special one. His name is Paul.

During our last home game of the regular season (Senior Night), Coach D. chose five seniors to start the game. Paul, another senior who always started, showing his unselfishness, gave me the honor of taking his place in the starting lineup. I was happy and thanked him for that. I did not want to let Paul or my teammates down, so I relished the moment and played an excellent game, scoring points, hustling on defense, dishing out several assists, and most of all, controlling my emotions.

My teaching assistant from BOCES, Ms. Friscina, along with my siblings and parents were in the crowd cheering me on. I was grateful for that opportunity. I felt free for the first time in a long time. Eventually, our team won that game, which most importantly, helped us clinch a playoff berth. I am forever thankful to the Mount Sinai School District for giving me the opportunity to redeem myself and play again as a fifth-year senior.

The basketball season eventually ended, and everything else in school was going well. I was now 19 years old and trying not to think about what could have been; I was focusing on what will be. I was a few months away from graduating. I was making good decisions in school and maturing out of school.

I was now being respectful to the staff and teachers at Mount Sinai that I used to give a hard time to. My classmates, on the other hand, were wondering why I had not graduated yet, as I would hear "old man" and other funny jokes shouted at me in the hallways. I did not take those jokes personally; plus, I knew those words did not matter because I was already beating the odds and proving the doubters wrong.

I overcame many trials and tribulations, especially in high school. That is what life is about: getting through the darkness and working hard and waiting patiently for the light to appear. On June 27, 2004, that light finally appeared. I looked up to heaven, gave thanks, and finally heard my name being called to receive my high school diploma. I received it and walked proudly back to my seat. The long, excruciating battle had finally ended in victory.

The struggles in high school were evident, but I never stopped persevering and eventually took pride in my schoolwork. I matured greatly and started taking advice from others, something I never did to begin my high school career. I could have dropped out and failed miserably. I realized those were selfish decisions, so I pressed on against all odds and heeded the advice of my family and educators to achieve success. I learned from my mistakes and was ready for the next chapter in my life.

<u>An Inspirational Quote for You</u>

"Success is not final; failure is not fatal: It is the courage to continue that counts."

—Winston Churchill

No matter how bad it got for me in high school, I continued to fight through the struggles. You too can overcome whatever life throws at you with a courageous mindset. Get back up every time you fail. The path I was on in school was an unconventional one, but nonetheless, I made it to the finish line. If your path changes unexpectedly, create a new path, accept the assistance of others, and make a difference. The obstacles for me were hard to overcome, but I refused to fail. So always remember: Persevere and never give up!

FIVE

Facing Death

This chapter will help you better understand some of the people I was associating with in high school. You will read about two near-death experiences that woke me up during my past. The stories you are about to read are honest and true, although some names were changed to protect their identity.

First Time Facing Death

It was a cool, breezy evening on October 8, 2001. I was only 16 years old and just wanted to have some fun. I was waiting patiently outside the house for my friend Chris to arrive so we could leave and enjoy the night. Approximately 20 minutes later, Chris arrived.

We left my house riding our bikes. About five minutes from my house is where our friend Harry lived, our next destination. When we arrived at Harry's house, we already had a plan in mind. We went there with some money, hoping to purchase some alcohol. Harry told us that he could not hang out but was willing to make a deal with us. I dug into my pocket, pulled out my money, and counted it. I had only $40 at the time, so I handed it all to Harry. He told Chris and me that he would give us two bottles of liquor in exchange for the $40; it was a deal. Chris and I were happy and ready to embark on our adventure.

We thanked Harry and quickly left his home excited and happy. With a bottle of liquor for each of us, we were contemplating a place to stay at so we could drink and hang out. Riding around in Mount Sinai (a conservative, rural town) on our bikes as young teens with bottles of liquor in our hands was a recipe for disaster. The sun was setting and darkness approached, so we had to make a quick decision as we were riding around the neighborhood now for 20 minutes. We were growing impatient and finally had a consensus: riding and drinking was the plan.

We stopped at a curb to open our bottles without anyone looking, or so we thought. Chris and I took a few swigs, said cheers, and waited for the first buzz to kick in. After drinking and sitting near our bikes on a corner for 10 minutes, it was now time to venture off again, but now we were feeling tipsy.

We closed up the bottles and continued riding our bikes around the town feeling free, without a worry in the world. There was still a small glimpse of daylight in the sky. We began driving faster, while trying to grasp our bottles tightly in one hand and a handlebar with the other hand. We never left our neighborhood, but it started to feel like a cross-country journey after consuming a lot of liquor. We did not stop drinking; in fact, we did not even stop riding in order to take sips out of our bottles.

It was now dark and becoming harder to ride and drink at the same time. Chris and I were having fun, but it seemed like he was having more fun. I was beginning to look and act extremely careless. By this time, I had finished more than half the bottle of liquor, and my slim body was starting to feel the effects. Chris asked me a few times if I was okay, and I responded, "Yea-a-a," with a slur in my voice.

We continued riding down other blocks in the neighborhood, which were very dark with few streetlights. My bike was starting to feel wobbly and unsteady. I thought I had a flat tire or a screw loose. I realized the bike mechanically was fine, and it was my drunkenness that was causing all the problems. I started swerving all over the street while Chris was trying to get my attention, but I heard nothing. As I continued to peddle trying to stay focused, I stopped suddenly, hit the curb, and immediately lost consciousness.

Chris jumped off his bike and hurried to where I had crashed, trying to wake me up. Minutes later, other people who lived nearby came over to see what all the commotion was about. 9-1-1 was dialed immediately after several attempts to revive me had failed. My older brother Mark was also called, and he hurried over to the scene, as we lived just a few blocks away.

I was not moving, and my face showed no signs of improvement. The ambulance took approximately ten minutes to arrive. When they finally arrived, they worked quickly, trying to regain my consciousness. After another failed attempt to regain my consciousness, they put me on a stretcher, into the ambulance, and hurried me off to John T. Mather Hospital, a short distance from the scene.

Mark was furious. He had several questions and wanted answers fast. Chris had all the answers. He explained to my brother what had happened in a shocked and sad tone. He told my brother where we got the alcohol, what we were doing, and how much I had to drink. Mark, with all the information he needed, called my parents and hurried off to the hospital.

Mark met my parents there around 9:00 p.m. and told them what happened. My mother and father were angry and worried at the same time. In the meantime, the doctors were pumping nearly a bottle of liquor out of my stomach. My parents called home to give the rest of the family an update on my present condition.

After a tough procedure, the doctors had finally finished pumping all the fluids out of my stomach. Mark and my parents were now allowed to visit me. When they arrived in my hospital room, I was weak but semi-conscious. I could not see their faces clearly, but I am sure they were not happy. After my brother had seen that I was all right, he headed home. My parents stayed at the hospital until I woke up at 3:00 a.m.

With my eyes blurry and my body aching, I finally woke up from the scariest night of my life, a nightmare that had turned out to be real. I was wearing a gown from the hospital. (I must have thrown up and/or urinated all over my clothes, so the hospital personnel had to change me.) My parents were staring me right in the eyes. I was shocked when I saw them and still did not fully realize what had happened, so they filled me in.

They were disappointed by my actions. I had failed them once again as a teenager. They did not say much; instead, they let me collect myself to think about my actions, knowing I would hear it from them for days and weeks to come. I put on the clean clothes my parents had brought and could not wait to go home. I was embarrassed to even walk out of the hospital with the thought of all the personnel involved in my emergency procedure looking at me.

The ride home was an awkward and depressing one. I could not wait to fall asleep and forget about what had transpired over the last ten hours. The short ride home felt like an eternity. It finally came to an end, as we pulled into our driveway in the early hours of the morning.

I woke up the next day and met with my parents to discuss a severe punishment. They decided to ground me for a month, and I was not able to use the phone. I deserved it and could not complain. My actions that night were selfish. I almost died not thinking about anyone that night but myself. This happened a few months before transitioning to Eastern Suffolk BOCES.

Second Time Facing Death

The next near-death experience happened toward the end of my high school career. It was a cool, summer night and my friend Johnny wanted to hang out. We called up a few of our friends who also wanted to hang out. Johnny and I picked them up and then proceeded to Johnny's big, luxurious house in Mount Sinai. Before arriving at our destination, we made a quick pit stop at 7-11 to pick up some food and alcohol. We picked up all we needed and continued on to Johnny's house.

At the time, Johnny was living with his parents and his younger sister who were not home too often, so we had the entire house to ourselves that night. The environment was perfect, plus the fact that Johnny and I were hanging out with two attractive girls. We were relaxing and drinking, without a care in the world. As the night continued, the fun continued. The weather was beautiful, so we stayed outside.

After a few hours of drinking, the girls asked us to drive them home. We cleaned up our mess quickly and headed toward Johnny's car. We all were so intoxicated that no one worried or questioned Johnny's ability to drive. I got in the back seat with Amanda (the girl I was hanging out with) and off we went to drive the girls home. They too lived in Mount Sinai, so the ride was short. Johnny seemed to be driving well considering his condition. We made it passed a few lights and long blocks and entered into Amanda's neighborhood. Shortly thereafter, we arrived at Amanda's house where both girls were dropped off. After getting them home safely, it was time for me and Johnny to go home.

We began heading back toward our neighborhood, and I was starting to feel nervous. Johnny's driving ability seemed worse than before. He started dazing off behind the wheel. I kept asking Johnny if he was good to continue driving, and he kept replying, "Yea, I am good," in a hesitant, stubborn tone.

We continued on our journey home, cutting through some back roads, trying to avoid the open roads and police. We then were coming up a narrow and winding road and quickly approached a four-way intersection. Johnny, now driving aggressively, was heading toward a glaring red light. Another car was driving past the intersection, but their light was green. I kept quiet, assuming that Johnny realized our light was red. Without a chance to think or say something to Johnny…BANG! We collided with an incoming car, dead smack in the middle of the intersection.

Some spectators in the vicinity came running toward the scene to see what had happened. My friend Melvin, who was working at a nearby restaurant, recognized Johnny's car and started sprinting toward the scene of the accident. The police and ambulance were called immediately, and sirens were heard within minutes. Johnny's car was completely wrecked. Johnny and I were now lying on opposite ends of the street. Although we were both beat up a bit, miraculously, we were still breathing.

Johnny, feeling dazed and realizing what he had just done, went rushing over to the person in the other car who we crashed into, seeing if she was all right. Thankfully, she was fine and shockingly not too upset. Feeling guilty, Johnny ran over to me, made sure I was fine, and apologized. He was so paranoid and did not know what to do. Johnny then asked me for a piece of gum to cover up the smell of alcohol on his breath. I gave him a piece of gum and threw a piece in my mouth, too.

The ambulance arrived first and one of the medics noticed right away that I was nursing my left leg. The lady quickly cut my pant leg and tended to the gash. She then recommended that I go to the hospital for precautionary reasons. I refused at first but then decided to go. It was best to leave the scene as quickly as possible.

The police arrived shortly after the ambulance did to make sure everyone was okay. Surprisingly, the police did not notice anything unusual or suspicious. Johnny was especially lucky that the police did not question him, or worse off, give him a breathalyzer test to see if he was driving under the influence. He dangerously put our lives and someone else's life in jeopardy. With that said, I should have been more forceful in stopping him from driving.

I stayed in the hospital for about a half hour to get the gash on my leg treated. Then I called my parents to pick me up. I explained to them what happened on the ride back home. Although they were upset at me for drinking, they knew Johnny was the one to make the wrong choice to drive. Johnny called me later that night apologizing. Bottom line, we were both fortunate to still be alive. And for me, my second time facing death was another close call.

An Inspirational Quote for You

"In the blink of an eye, everything could change. So, forgive often and love with all your heart. You never know when you might not have that chance again."

—Author Unknown

When you are going through a tough time, tragedy, or even a near-death experience like I encountered, do not be foolish and do nothing; instead, make changes and do everything. Do everything possible to help yourself overcome the adversity, and if you get through the experience, then truly learn from it and develop a new plan and course of action to turn back onto the straight road. This chapter should also teach you to keep your loved ones close and not to hold grudges, as you never know when your time will be up.

Six

LET'S GO: Time to Teach

A cademically, I finished off my high school career in such remarkable fashion that I decided to attend college immediately in the fall. In September 2004, three months after graduating high school, I applied and got accepted to Suffolk County Community College (S.C.C.C.). This school is a two-year community college located in Selden, New York. I signed up for four classes and was officially in college. I never thought I would walk onto a college campus, but in September 2004, that dream became a reality.

I was extremely motivated and focused when I attended S.C.C.C. My mother was still there helping me to study for my tests and complete my papers, and my father was still there giving me spiritual strength. It felt so good to attend college. Now, at age 20, I was feeling successful and planning my future. After completing a successful first year at S.C.C.C., I finally chose a career. Of course, it was none other than education. Seeing what my amazing mother did for me when I was younger inspired me to make that career choice.

My second and final year at S.C.C.C. was a success like the first year. I was focused and worked hard every day to prevail in all my classes. The hard work and sleepless nights of studying and writing paid off. The perseverance I showed helped me achieve success, graduating in the summer of August 2006 with an associate degree. Receiving my first college diploma was gratifying, but now I had to decide what I wanted to do next.

I had to make a quick decision because my last summer class finished in August and the college fall semester would be starting in a few weeks. I used the next few days to contemplate my decision. I spoke to my parents, looked into a few schools, and came to a final decision a week later.

I chose Dowling College. My mother wanted me to be happy and comfortable, so she drove me to the school to apply and sign the mandatory paperwork. I was feeling good about my decision and ready to officially become a student at Dowling College. The major I chose was "Elementary Education." My journey to become a teacher, following in the footsteps of my mother, had officially begun.

Dowling College is located in Oakdale, New York, about 30 minutes from my home in Mount Sinai. I was now a few weeks into my first semester at Dowling College. I was around other college students with ambitions of becoming a teacher like me. The professors were noteworthy and knowledgeable. I was now enjoying life and working hard to become a teacher.

Most of my credits from S.C.C.C. transferred over to Dowling, which was good, but now there were more required classes and student-teaching assignments that needed to be completed in order to successfully obtain my bachelor's degree. I did not want to be overwhelmed, so I only signed up for three classes my first semester at Dowling. It was a good idea since I was still learning the ropes and becoming familiar with all the educational terms. I finished all the required work, and in no time, breezed through the first semester with grades at or above a B.

There was more work to be done, though, and I still had a lot of doubt about becoming a teacher. I had come a long way but did not know if I could actually teach in front of students. Nonetheless, I kept at it and flourished through the spring 2007 semester.

The second semester at Dowling College was also a success, as I obtained 12 more credits. My first year at Dowling College was officially over. I had successfully completed two semesters, along with a few more summer classes. After that first year at Dowling, I started looking and searching for a girlfriend. People always told me not to "search for love," but I couldn't help it. My second year at Dowling started in September of 2007. I was still concentrating on my schoolwork and the process of becoming a teacher, but the thought of having that significant other in my life was appealing.

The 2007 fall semester went smoothly without any issues or setbacks. I was also working a few times per week at Tutor Time, a day-care center. I started working there in August 2006. Like my education classes at Dowling College, the day care was filled with females. As time passed in school and working at the day care, I eventually found what I was looking for.

After the semester ended, I focused my attention on this girl who I worked with at Tutor Time. Her name was Nicole. She seemed nice and was attractive, but she was already in a two-year relationship with another guy. My co-workers at Tutor Time began telling me that Nicole was not being treated well by her boyfriend and that she was not happy. That made me even more attracted to Nicole because I knew I would treat her with respect if I had the chance. My relentless pursuit of Nicole carried on, and in December of 2007, things became serious between us.

I was talking to Nicole as much as I could at work and even gave her my number, hoping she would text or call me to talk. She was reluctant at first to take my number down because of her "controlling" boyfriend, but Nicole also knew that they were not doing well together. She put my number in her phone, but under the name "Danielle" instead of "Daniel," just in case her boyfriend looked through her phone.

We hung out a few times that December and quickly started to enjoy each other's company. Nicole was all but done with her boyfriend and we both knew it. A few weeks later in December, they officially broke up. It gave me some relief to know that Nicole was a single woman, and if I played my cards right, we would be able to begin a relationship.

The next month went well getting to know Nicole more, along with signing up for my first semester of student teaching. At first, I couldn't find a student teaching placement, but like always, my mother lent her helping hand. She was currently working in the Sachem School District as a reading teacher. She mentioned my name to her administration for a position as a student teacher for the upcoming spring semester. She got back to me quickly with the thumbs up. I was ready to teach for the first time, at Waverly Elementary School, in Holbrook, New York. This experience began in January 2008.

I met with my cooperating teacher to go over my student teaching assignment and was anxious and ready to get started. She knew my mother already, which made me happy and less nervous. My cooperating teacher was a first grade teacher. She had only four students with autism in her self-contained class. I was ready to learn how to become a successful teacher and see if this was what I actually wanted to do in life. Along with student teaching, I was still going to school at Dowling College full-time, so things in my life were busy and hectic.

Finally, the day had come: my first observation; my first real teaching experience. Using all my resources and going over the lesson with my mother countless times the night before, I was ready to teach for the first time in my life. I was extremely nervous and just wanted the observation to go well. My observer went over a few things with me outside of the classroom, then I proceeded back into the classroom to teach my lesson.

Since students with autism learn best in one-on-one settings, I only had to teach one student the lesson that I prepared. I worked hard to make the lesson developmentally appropriate. It was a matching lesson, but I made sure to make it easy enough to prevent the student from getting easily frustrated. It was a short lesson, and I kept the student engaged using tons of positive reinforcement. Twenty minutes later, the lesson was done, and I knew deep down that it was a success. All the planning, studying, and help from my mother and cooperating teacher had paid off.

My observer asked to speak with me outside the class to go over the lesson. After hearing my observer's first few words, I was relieved. She enjoyed the lesson and said I showed "good composure" and reacted appropriately when there were distractions. I was ecstatic and filled with joy. I could not wait to tell my family. The next three observations were also a success, and I was gaining confidence as a teacher. The 2008 spring semester had ended, as well as my second full year at Dowling College.

I went into the summer of 2008 encouraged and stress free. I did not sign up for any summer classes for the first time in my college career. All of the summer classes I had taken in high school, along with all the summer classes I had voluntarily taken at S.C.C.C., were enough. I needed a real summer break. I was also in love for the first time in my life. I was feeling great emotionally and physically; the days of depression and destruction were gone.

Nicole and I spent every day together that summer. We officially started dating on April 5, 2008. I took her into New York City, and after that night, we were officially a couple. We were getting along so well that we planned a trip to Cabo San Lucas, Mexico. The summer of 2008 and that trip to Mexico were unbelievable. My parents were happy for me. After that summer ended, I had to prepare quickly for my final year at Dowling and get ready to begin my second student-teaching experience.

That semester I student taught at Accompsett Elementary School in Smithtown, NY. My cooperating teacher was extremely supportive on my first day, which helped ease the nervousness I was feeling. This was a different experience than last semester's experience because it was a general education classroom. There were 25 students in this class and only four students had a disability. The first few days were overwhelming, but my cooperating teacher and all the students enjoyed my presence, which made me feel comfortable. The irony of this teaching experience was that the student who I worked with the most had the same disability that I had in school.

The student's name was Michael, and I will never forget Michael. He was a challenging student, but we worked well together to promote positive behaviors. Michael and I got along very well and eventually my cooperating teacher had me work with Michael one-on-one because she knew I had a good rapport with him.

There were many words and sayings posted on the walls in her classroom, but there was one word that stood out the most, and one that I knew all too well. The word was perseverance. I decided to put it to good use for Michael. I ripped a piece of paper out of his notebook and cut that piece of paper in half. I wrote the word PERSEVERANCE on it in big, bold letters. Then, at the bottom of the paper I wrote, Michael, never give up! I took some tape and placed it on his desk, and the rest was history. Whenever he started getting upset or stating that he "could not do it," referring to an assignment, I would point to the piece of paper I created for him, and in an encouraging voice reply, "Yes, you can do it, Michael!" I gave Michael some other words of advice in the heat of the moment, and that was all he needed to stay on task and believe again.

The rest of that semester went well with support from my cooperating teacher, and of course, my mother. I received excellent feedback on all my observations. I was down to one semester and one more student-teaching experience until I could graduate college. The place I chose to student teach at for my last semester was an interesting choice, to say the least.

It was now late in December 2008, and I had trouble finding a student teaching placement. I exhausted all my options, except for one I did not even think of at first. At the time, my mother was working as an administrator for Eastern Suffolk BOCES. I did not know if that was where I wanted to student teach at, but I did not have much time left to decide. My mother told me that she would inquire about a student teaching placement in one of the elementary schools within BOCES.

A few weeks later, the placement coordinator at BOCES informed me that there were some openings for student teachers. I was thrilled and relieved because I only had a few weeks left before my last college semester began. Finally, the decision was made.

The school I was placed in was Masera Learning Center in West Islip, New York. This was my third and final student teaching experience. This was the ultimate test on whether I truly wanted to become a teacher or not. It was ironic knowing the school that would determine my possible fate as a teacher, was part of Eastern Suffolk BOCES, a program I knew all too well from my high school days.

It was the end of January and the semester had started. The class I was placed in was one of the highest functioning classes in the school. The classroom teacher, Mrs. K., was very supportive and let me work one-on-one with each student, so I could learn and gain knowledge about different aspects of the autism spectrum. Because the class was high functioning, my first lesson was a whole-class lesson. Mrs. K. helped me prepare and gave me all the pointers I needed to succeed. A month into my student-teaching experience, my first observation had finally come. I did a fun and engaging lesson on telling time.

All the students responded well to the lesson, and the feedback I got from that lesson was encouraging. My first lesson was a success, and I was gaining confidence by the day. I had only three more lessons left to teach before I was done working as a student teacher.

M.L.C. had other student teachers that semester and they wanted each of us to have diverse experiences in different classrooms. This meant that I would have to leave the class I was in and student teach in another class. In March, halfway through the semester, I said my goodbyes and moved on to the other class.

The teacher's name was Mrs. B. She was also a great teacher. From day one, Mrs. B. made me feel comfortable in her class. I was just trying to fit in and do whatever I was asked to do. I only needed one observation in this class. There were a few weeks left in the semester and it was time to teach my fourth and final lesson. Ms. B. gave me advice on how to carry out the lesson, while keeping the students attentive and engaged. Thanks to her support and my mother's encouragement, my final lesson as a student teacher was a success, a victory once and for all. I now realized that teaching was definitely the career choice I wanted.

The spring semester flew by, and May was here in no time. I finished off my college career at Dowling College with a GPA of 2.7. I thought this was a pretty good GPA for a former special education student. This was the end of a long journey. I handed in all my writing papers on time and took a few final exams. One week later, an unbelievable day had finally arrived.

On May 16, 2009, I received the college diploma I had been yearning for. Right before I heard my name announced, I glanced up at the sky to thank the Lord and walked proudly toward the president of Dowling College to receive my diploma. The walk back to my seat was a special one. My family, along with my grandma and Aunt Annie in attendance, were screaming my name and waving me down on my walk back to my seat. Not only was I now a college graduate, but I was also a certified New York State teacher. The search for a teaching job had officially begun.

The summer of 2009 was a relaxing one, but unfortunately, a sad summer as well. I made sure to relax as much as possible, but it was difficult to do. I was not working or going to school, which was rare for a summer in my life, and my relationship with Nicole was beginning to unravel. She was traveling back and forth from New York City to Long Island a few days a week for school, and we were not seeing each other as much as we once had.

I was also hanging out with my friends more. Of course, I was not cheating on her, but she was starting to have doubts about our relationship. That summer I sometimes went days without seeing Nicole, and when I did, it was late at night; I would go to her house, her parents and sister would be sleeping, and we would just fight. She would cry and tell me how her mother "missed" me and how I had "changed." That made me sad because I was close with her mother and family. Nicole's mother was also battling cancer at the time and her father was fighting his own personal issues, which made things more difficult for Nicole.

In the summer of 2008, we were expressing love in Mexico, and in the summer of 2009, we were struggling to keep our love alive. We used to watch movies like Pearl Harbor, but during the summer of 2009, we did not watch one movie together.

After all the fights and arguments, the time had finally come. In August 2009, Nicole and I had officially broken up. We mutually agreed to "take a break" and possibly try again in the near future. Nicole was heartbroken. I was trying to soak everything in and was wondering where it all went wrong.

Her family was sad about the breakup because I used to babysit Nicole's little cousins with her and was close with her aunts and uncles. Nicole had a small extended family, but they were fun and loving to be around. Her mother was like a second mother to me; I missed her greatly. My family also loved Nicole, and they were all sad that we had broken up.

The rest of that summer was depressing and stressful. I was applying for teaching jobs and fighting with Nicole every night. Toward the end of that summer, Nicole wanted to try again, but I still was not ready. I needed "more time." Eventually, Nicole started dating another guy. When that happened, I started getting jealous, and there was nothing I could do about it. She gave me multiple chances, but I did not feel it would work out between us, so we both stopped trying.

We kept a picture book when we were dating of our memories and all the places we had visited together. After we broke up, Nicole gave it back to me. I looked through it again, and when I got to the last page, I noticed something different. There was a picture of us, and a note written near the picture along with a sad face that read: "Good things always come to an end." I choked up inside after reading this line.

The summer that started with much joy and promise, ended with much uncertainty and emotional stress. Even with all the sadness and guilt I was feeling toward my breakup with Nicole, I knew I had to refocus and find a teaching job. Overall, I was still happy to call myself a college graduate.

After getting through the emotional summer of 2009, it was now time to start working again. As for Nicole and me, we grew farther apart, and all hope was lost. We were officially done. We remained friends, but we had to let each other go for good. Getting a job was now my number one priority.

I applied to several teaching jobs during the summer of 2009 but to no avail. Then September came, and my mother surprised me with some good news. She told me that Eastern Suffolk BOCES was hiring substitute teachers for the school year; I was ecstatic. I called to set up an interview and gathered together all the information I needed to prepare for it. A week later, I went to the interview. The interview went well, and I got a call back a few days later notifying me that I was officially hired as a substitute teacher. It was where I belonged.

The irony of it all was incredible. I once was lost as a student with disabilities, then fast forward to the beginning of my career, I was teaching students with disabilities. I left BOCES in 2004 as a student, and five years later, I returned with the roles reversed, as the teacher.

My first year I worked predominately as a substitute teacher for BOCES before getting a permanent position as a teaching assistant at one of their schools (Jefferson Academic Center). Officially, I worked for BOCES until March 2013 and then began a temporary position in the Bayport School

District for the remainder of the 2012-2013 school year. After my position there was "excessed," I returned to BOCES and a few other school districts for the next two school years, working as a substitute teacher.

All the teaching experiences at BOCES and a few other school districts helped me to develop the tools I needed to become a successful teacher. Most importantly, I gained confidence, which I knew was needed in order to be an effective and inspirational teacher. All I needed now was a full-time teaching job.

<u>An Inspirational Quote for You</u>

"I am only one, but still I am one. I cannot do everything, but still I can do something. And because I cannot do everything, I will not refuse to do the something that I can do."

—Hellen Keller

In college, I didn't get the best grades, but I obtained good enough grades. Initially, I was a poor public speaker, but then I improved. I tried, and failed, but kept on trying until I eventually succeeded and achieved my goals.

You too can achieve anything if you truly believe. Stop being pessimistic, waiting for negative things to happen, and instead be optimistic, knowing and believing that positive things will happen. Do not worry about being some famous Hollywood star; instead, worry about being the best you can be in your own Hollywood life. Listen to your heart and not to what you hear or see on television. Believe in yourself, and you too will become successful at something one day.

SEVEN

The Worst Day of My Life

I was starting to get frustrated teaching as a substitute year after year. It was now 2015, and I felt that I had deserved a true teaching job with my own classroom. During the 2014-2015 school year, I landed a leave replacement position as a teacher in the Riverhead Central School District, teaching sixth grade. Although it was a great experience filled with lots of success, the position ended in March of 2015, so I had to go back to substitute teaching for the remainder of that school year.

I applied to a few teaching jobs before summer vacation began, but I did not get any job offers. Right after the school year ended, like I did the previous three summers, I headed off to Kent, Connecticut, where I was working as a camp counselor at KenMont Camp. This is a sleepaway camp, so the campers and counselors are required to stay at camp for the entire summer.

The summer of 2015 at camp was amazing, as I got to see my friends from the previous three summers, along with the opportunity to meet new people from literally all over the world. But I was still stressed out that I could not find a teaching job. It was tough paying the bills each year as a substitute teacher. It was also difficult to apply for jobs while working at camp because the counselors had only a limited amount of time away from the campers.

Finally, after applying to a few more jobs, I got a call to teach a demo lesson in the Riverhead Central School District in August of 2015. I had a good feeling about this job opportunity, especially after teaching there just months earlier in a position as a leave replacement teacher. I studied hard for my demo lesson while I was at camp and then headed home on August 9, so I could teach my demo lesson the following day. My boss at camp allowed me to travel home for the day, but I had to return right after my lesson as there was still more than a week left of camp.

After sleeping home for the first time in two months, I woke up the next morning and was focused and determined to get this job. I headed to Riverhead and arrived shortly before 9:00 a.m. Overall, the lesson was a success. I did not feel too nervous because I had worked so hard to make sure I was prepared for the moment. Right after I finished teaching the lesson, I headed straight back to camp. I called my mother on the way back to camp and told her about the demo lesson. She was happy and relayed the good news to the rest of my family.

A few days later, I received a call at camp from Riverhead on Wednesday morning, August 13. They offered me a job as a full-time teacher in sixth grade on a tenure track, and of course, I happily accepted the position! The long six-year journey of substitute teaching was finally over.

August 19 was officially my last day as a counselor at summer camp. It was also my campers' last year at the camp. They were the oldest division in camp: Dodos. I got the privilege of having Dodos for both sessions at camp that summer.

My time spent with them over a four-year period was unbelievable. Whether it was the intense basketball games with my campers and our late-night conversations, or even the nonstop jokes, being their counselor was awesome. I also got to hold the highest honor during the last week of the first session at camp as "General" of Color War. During Color War, the camp is split up between two teams: grey and blue. I was blessed and had the privilege of being the General for the Blue Policemen. And on the other hand, one of my best friends at camp, Howie, just so happened to be the General of the grey team: The Grey Firefighters.

Then came my session-two campers. I was always eager to see them when they arrived in July. I will always remember the fun games played in our bunks, the songs that pumped us up, and the unexpected trip to see one of my campers compete for Connecticut in the 2015 Little League World Series. Those times were priceless, and I will hold onto them forever.

Although the summer of 2015 at camp was unforgettable, I was tired and could not wait to go home. I said goodbye to all my campers and co-counselors. Like usual, I got asked to chaperon for some campers who were traveling back home via LaGuardia Airport in New York. After finishing up my duties as a chaperon, I was ready to go home, which was only an hour from the airport.

Wednesday, August 19, 2015

7:38 p.m. – As I was getting ready to leave the airport, my brother Mark called me to say hi. We spoke for about 10 minutes, and he started off by congratulating me on my new job and welcoming me home. After catching up on life, my brother in a calm voice told me, "Daddy got into a little accident...." I was a little nervous, but Mark reassured me that our dad was okay and that he did not even crash into another car. I was happy to hear the good news and was now on my way home from the airport. One of my best friends from camp, Markel, met me at the airport to come home with me for the night because his flight back home to Detroit was not until the next day. As we were finally leaving the airport, I got another call, this time from my mother.

7:49 p.m. – She too welcomed me home and gave me some more details about my father's accident. My mother told me that "Daddy has a few cracked ribs" and some injuries, but she did not think the injuries were too bad. My mother then told me that she had to get off the phone because the doctors were looking to speak with her again at the hospital.

7:55 p.m. – Now I was getting very curious, so I gave my mother a call to see what the doctors had just told her. This time she did not sound as optimistic. My mother said the doctors are seeing "what they can do," but her voice seemed much different than the conversation we had just minutes earlier. I told her to keep me posted, then I hung up the phone. On the way home, I briefly told my friend Markel what happened with my father and then we started talking about our great summer at camp.

8:23 p.m. – I got another call, and it was my mother again. She was hysterical, telling me, "It is not good, it is not good! Hurry, come to the hospital! Daddy might not make it!" Then I responded, "What hospital?" in a shocked and angry voice. After my mother told me what hospital, I quickly hung up the phone and rushed there, as I was still 40 minutes away. I wept in silence the entire ride there. Markel knew by the phone call what was going on, so he did not say a word. I was driving 90 mph on the Long Island Expressway, trying my best to get to the hospital as quickly as I could. I now feared the worst: My father, my best friend, could be gone forever.

9:05 p.m. – Markel and I finally arrived at the hospital. I parked quickly, and we ran as fast as we could into the hospital. I saw people from our church when we entered the hospital, but I bypassed them all, looking to see my father and no one else. I ran into the emergency room and saw my mother, Lauren, and Maria sitting down and waiting nervously. I took a seat and broke down crying. I sat with my face down, waiting to see my father.

The doctors performed a procedure to minimize the internal bleeding, and the following update was positive. They were putting tubes in his chest to help him breathe better through his lungs, which were severely injured during the accident. There was progress being made, and my mother made sure to fill me in with the good news: "Daniel, he is doing better. They are going to put the tube in him and then he will be okay…."

Later that night, things were looking so much better that the doctors decided to move my father out of the emergency room and into another room in the hospital. I was so happy to hear the good news. It was now midnight, and I was ready to finally go home. Plus, tomorrow was my big day; the day I finally got to sign my first teacher contract. The rest of my family stayed at the hospital a little longer to make sure our father got to his new room okay.

Thursday, August 20, 2015

8:00 a.m. – The next morning, I woke up feeling happy. I was ready to go sign my contract and then excited to visit my father in the hospital afterward. With the thought of visiting my father running through my mind, I finally arrived at Riverhead Central School District and signed my contract and paperwork as quickly as I could.

8:30 a.m. – I left the school district and arrived at the hospital shortly after 9:00 a.m. Happy as ever, I walked up to the front desk and asked them what room number my father was in. They told me his room number but said that "visiting hours do not start until 11:00 a.m." I was thinking to myself, *Are you kidding me?* I refrained from commenting back and politely took a seat to wait until visiting hours began.

9:35 a.m. – Christy at the time was in Florida on vacation and was doing all she could pleading at an airport to get a flight home. After exchanging a few text messages with her about when she was coming home, I told her that I was at the hospital and about to visit our father. I then text messaged Christy once again to update her in case she was not told yet: "I am at the hospital, about to visit Daddy. He was doing better last night, so they moved him to a room...."

A few minutes later, I received a group text message from a number that was not saved in my phone. I did not know who it was, but it was sent to my mother and siblings, so I figured it was someone close to our family. It was my cousin's wife. I did not understand the text message at first and thought it was all wrong. I was very confused, so I read it a second time to fully understand it. "I am so sorry for your loss...." It just looked like a long paragraph telling our family about someone who had passed away. I was so confused.

I still did not fully understand the text message. Then, Christy called me minutes later probably because she was confused about the text messages that I was sending to her with updates about our father. She knew what had happened, and I certainly did not. When I picked up her phone call, Christy was crying hysterically and told me that "Daddy did not make it." I did not need to know anything else. I was so upset and crushed inside. My mind was racing. *Why didn't anyone tell me? What happened to my father?* The doctors told us that he was fine. (Later on, I found out that no one in my family told me that my father had passed away just hours earlier that morning because they wanted me to get through signing my important paperwork and teacher contract without going crazy.)

I stormed out of the hospital with my body weak and tears dripping down my face. I drove home while Christy stayed on the phone with me. She wanted me to get home safely. I just wanted to see my father; but in the blink of an eye, he was gone. The aftermath was terrible.

Thursday, August 20, 2015, was the worst day of my life. When I got home, I yelled and broke down, while everyone else who was home already knew the details of what happened. My siblings, my Uncle Billy, Lauren's husband, and my mother consoled and comforted me saying, "Everything will be okay," although I knew it would not. I never imagined something like this could happen, especially to the strongest man I knew. But it really did happen. I thought things like this could only happen in dreams or movies.

After mourning with my family in the living room for an hour, I went to my bedroom and passed out for several hours. Later that day and the next day, our family and friends flooded the house to give us strength. The following days were obviously tough for us, but we were reminded that our father was an unbelievable man, as many people came to show their respects at his funeral.

The weeks and months that followed were very difficult for me at work. I really just pretended to be happy when I was at work because I had no choice. But God gave me peace during that time, and he has helped me to persevere, even to this day. As I was still mourning five months after his passing, I decided to write my father a letter on February 1, 2016.

> Dear Dad,
> I miss you so much. I wish you were still here, but I know you are in a better place. I hope Heaven is treating you well. I cannot wait to go there, but like you always said, "I still have lots of work to do here on Earth first." Life is so hard to live without you. You were my leader and my best friend. You taught me how to build and fix things, and I am forever thankful for that. I know that knowledge will help me when I have my own house.
>
> I pretend to be happy at work and also when I am around our family and friends, but I am really sad and damaged inside. When I go home, there is no faking the happiness; it is all sadness and thoughts of you. As I think about it, though, and recall the amazing man you were, it is really all happy tears. It is hard to do things around the house without you there by my side, but when I think about you, just the thought of you gives me the strength to overcome the difficult tasks.
>
> I am so glad you were still here to know I had finally gotten that full-time teaching job I worked hard for. I know you were so happy for me. Everyone told me you were crying "tears of joy" when you heard the great news. Teaching full-time is unbelievable. It is lots of hard work, but I am up for the challenge. I have 27 amazing sixth graders who bring me joy. I am so blessed to be their teacher and will strive to be the best teacher I can be and know you are cheering me on.
>
> I miss hanging out with you and Mom; those were my favorite times. All our laughs, deep conversations on serious issues, and even when we used to fool around with Mom, were the best times. Remember the time when you were making

popcorn for yourself and Mom, and you played a joke on her? You walked back in the room with your popcorn and then you handed Mom her popcorn in the tiniest bowl with just a little popcorn in it as a joke. She totally believed that was all she was getting until you walked up to her a few minutes later with a normal-size bowl filled with popcorn. I will never forget those good times.

I will always remember Mom telling me when you were still here, "You are just like Daddy." And also, once in a while saying to you, "You are just like Daniel. You two are so alike!" I remember those times when Mom would get a little annoyed at us, but in those moments, that is when I started to realize how cool it actually was to be just like you.

I know it is a little weird, but I am sending you this letter in the mail, addressed to "Heaven," hoping you will somehow receive it, and if possible, send me a sign to let me know you received the letter. You know, kind of like when little Anthony saw an angel a few years ago and told Aunt Renee and Uncle Bobby who he actually saw: Uncle Tony. That is what I am hoping for.

With all this said, I want you to know that I love you so much and think about you every day. We all miss you so much. Mom really misses you but is staying strong. I will protect her for you. Please watch over us until we meet again.

Love,

Daniel

The crazy thing about sending this letter out addressed to Heaven (besides the fact that I was crazy for sending it out in the mail) is that it never was "Returned to Sender." I checked the mail for weeks but saw no returned mail. I was amazed, but then I thought, I have seen miracles before, so this was just another miracle. I truly believe the letter somehow found its way to my father. Maybe I am crazy, but where else could the letter have gone?

It was rough teaching during that school year and these last few years, but I have always reminded myself and my students that "everyone is going through a struggle." I have not told my students in any of the years teaching that I lost my father. I did not want people to feel bad for me. Whether it is a loss of a family member, a divorce, a personal or financial struggle, we are all going through some type of difficulty in life. The point is that we have to pick ourselves up and persevere through it because it will make us stronger in the end.

In June 2015 before I was heading off to camp that summer, my father had taken me out to eat at a local diner. He took me out to thank me for all the work I had done around the house and to say one last goodbye before I left. Like the years prior leaving for camp, I thought that night was just another normal night before heading off to camp for two months. I did not realize it would be our last fellowship together.

That dinner reminded me of "The Last Supper" Jesus had with his disciples before he was crucified. Although I saw my father briefly when I came home on the night of August 9 for my demo lesson, the "Last Supper" in June two months earlier was our last true fellowship together.

An Inspirational Quote for You

"Everyone is going through a struggle."

I made sure after my father's death not to mope around looking for people to feel bad for me. That is not the way to handle a tragedy. Although I did have many sad moments and still do, my father would not want me to just live life all sad and distraught looking for excuses.

I do my best to stay positive and work hard. This is what we all have to do during a struggle. Whether it is homelessness, a death in the family, depression, a financial struggle, etc., we are all going through a struggle in life. We cannot look for people to feel bad for us or to sit around and do nothing. Instead, we need to pick ourselves up and work harder than we ever did before the struggle.

EIGHT

A Dream Come True

Although I was excited to finally get a teaching job, I was still heartbroken from losing my father. Two weeks after he died, my new job had officially begun. I now had to stay strong more than ever before.

Year 1

The first year teaching sixth grade in the Riverhead Central School District was somewhat of a blur at times for obvious reasons, but I still had a successful year and saw my sixth graders turn into amazing readers and writers. Most importantly, I made sure my sixth graders were taught good morals and values, so they could become productive members of society, showing respect and kindness toward others.

As a teacher, I believe my number one goal is to inspire and motivate my students to get them to believe in themselves. One of my students was inspired by my teaching style, so his mother wrote me a beautiful letter and also sent it to my administration and superintendent on Friday, June 10, 2016.

> Dear Administration and Superintendent:
> Another school year comes to a close and with that my last two children move up to Riverhead Middle School. As a parent, this is bittersweet, but I feel that I need to take the time to write this letter on behalf of my son, Joseph. He has had fabulous teachers in the district, as have my other two children,

but he never had the experience of a "newbie," until this year. While all of my son's "seasoned" teachers were great at what they did, they had time to work out the kinks, so I really cannot compare.

This year Joseph had the pleasure of being in Mr. Casamassa's class. He has learned so much from him both educationally and also as a positive role model. Joseph enjoyed learning this year and has put in effort that I have not seen before. I can give that credit to Mr. Casamassa. He has given my son food for thought for his future.

Some quotes from Joseph through the school year include: "Mom, Mr. Casamassa is nice to everyone!" "Mom, Mr. Casamassa wears a shirt and tie every day, except field day, but the next day he was back to shirt and tie." "Mom, I think Mr. Casamassa tricks us into learning stuff because he makes it fun." I am so pleased to have had my son in Mr. Casamassa's "first class." I wish him all the joy and success as he is not just a "teacher," but he is an educator that truly has a gift. I am so glad he has shared his gift with my son and maybe one day my son's dreams of being a teacher just like Mr. Casamassa will come true! Thank you.

Sincerely,
Joyce

That letter made me feel special. Joseph and his mother made my first year much easier, and I guess you can say I was rewarded at the end of the year since my administrators and superintendent got to hear what was going on in my class directly from a parent. I will never forget Joseph, my sixth graders, and my first year teaching. It was also an unbelievable year because of the fact that two of my sixth graders had also just lost their fathers before the school year started. We all were in the fight together.

After that year had ended, my administration gave me the option to stay there in sixth grade or teach third grade at another school in my school district. After a few days contemplating it, I decided to move down a few grades and teach third grade at Riley Avenue Elementary School.

Year 2

My first year teaching third grade was tough initially because the students were much younger than my sixth graders, but after adjusting to third grade, the year turned out to be a great success. My administration enjoyed having me there. The other teachers seemed to like me as well, but most of all, my students and their parents appreciated my unique teaching style.

I enjoyed every moment of that school year and teaching third grade. After completing the school year successfully, I knew this was the grade level that I wanted to teach for the rest of my career. After inspiring and motivating this group of third graders, along with collaborating and working with their parents, I was excited and ready for what else was in my future as a third grade teacher. Before the school year ended, a few parents wrote letters to me and my administration.

On the next few pages are two letters and a gift I received, which humbled me greatly. I will always remember this wonderful class.

> Dear Mr. Casamassa,
> We wanted to thank you for a truly great year. You are the benchmark for all teachers. I have four kids and honestly you are the most amazing teacher we have ever had. I cannot thank you enough for everything you do for these kids. They will all be better people for having someone like you in their life. I wish you a long, rewarding career. Thank you for everything you do and for being such an amazing role model. Have a great summer.
>
> > Sincerely,
> > Janet

And finally, before the school year ended…

> Good morning Mr. Casamassa,
> I wanted to thank you personally for taking the extra interest in James' third grade endeavor. You have made an impact on our son that will last a lifetime. Through your kindness and thoughtful approach to teaching, you have changed a young

boy's life. James left second grade frustrated and not wanting to attend school.

Although his grades were average, it was his inordinate displeasure that caught my attention each morning. We made adjustments at home but recognized the real change almost immediately from the start of the school year. Your encouragement from the outset made the difference for our son. Not only did James look forward to school each day, but he also wanted to do well to impress you. Your influence went further. He started asking to go to the park to play basketball, and he can now tell you about every player from the Bulls' 1990s dynasty squad, this, while learning to dribble with his left hand in our foyer.

So when you reflect on your own accomplishments this year, I would hope that you consider all the great things you have done for one young boy, which because of you, has a new outlook on learning. You are the differing factor and the adjustment that has helped James to not only progress, but you have also allowed him to shine. I will call administration to thank them personally for making you happen in our son's life. Thank you.

Sincerely,
James J.

On the next page is a beautiful gift I received that year from Donna, my "Class Mom." She was always quick to help me in class when we had special events and activities going on in school. She would always treat my students to delicious cupcakes and other snacks when she stopped in during the holidays. Most of all, she made me feel special at the end of the year by giving me this gift, which was signed by her amazing son Paulie and the rest of my wonderful students.

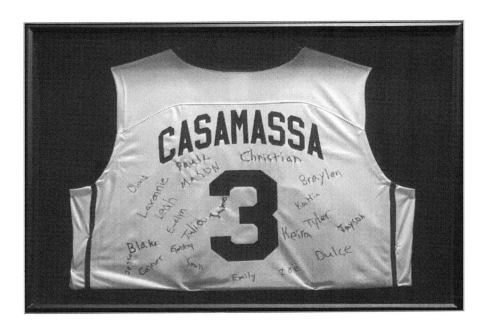

When I received the gift, I felt like a basketball player getting my jersey retired, except I was only in year two of teaching! I am thankful to this parent and her husband for coordinating the gift, along with the other parents who contributed financially.

I worked extremely hard my second year learning how to teach in a new grade. Although it was difficult at first, my students and their parents gave me the motivation to keep pressing on. After I successfully completed my second year teaching, I was able to enjoy the summer vacation with my family and friends.

Year 3

The 2017-2018 school year was much different than the previous two years because for the first time in my teaching career, I had English as a New Language (ENL) students in my class. These are students who grow up speaking a language other than English in their homes.

Although only six out of my 22 students in the class were ENL students, I still had to find different ways to teach them as they learned a new language. I made sure to motivate these students and help them to believe in themselves and feel confident as they learned English. I used pictures and engaging videos so they could learn the new material more effectively and efficiently, which was the turning point for them.

My non-ENL students were just as awesome, and they helped me to get through the year successfully. One of my students enjoyed my unique teaching style, so his parents decided to show their appreciation. They wrote me a nice letter early in the year and included my principal on the email.

> Dear Mr. Casamassa,
> My wife and I just wanted to send a quick little thank you for the work you have done with our son Brayden so far this year. He has had great teachers every year at Riley, but this year he is truly inspired to go to school and do his work. He comes home every day and tells us everything he has learned. My wife and I have been teachers for fifteen years, so we know the challenges that each school year brings. Thank you again for creating such a wonderful classroom environment for our son. If we can help in any way, please let us know.
>
> Best regards,
> Brett and Stephanie

My students helped me complete another amazing year teaching. On top of all the success I had that year, my students put the icing on the cake by performing at a high level on the NYS ELA Assessments, which is given to students in grades 3-8 toward the end of each school year. Although this is a highly publicized and politicized test, I always make sure not to worry about the politics of the test. I just try to prepare all my students for the test, and most of all, train them to believe in themselves and understand that through hard work and perseverance, all things are possible.

That year was special for me as it relates to this test because along with several of my students that year, two out of my six ENL students ended up getting 3s on the test. (Obtaining a 3 on the test is the benchmark, although receiving a "high 2" is also considered a good score, especially for ENL students.) During that school year, only 9.2% of ENL students in New York State achieved a score of 3 or better on this assessment (scores range from 1-4, with 4 being the highest score). Against all odds, I was very proud of what my ENL students accomplished that year.

I believed in all my students that year, which included my ENL students, and knew they were destined for greatness on this test. At times, I hear educators speaking about this test and ENL students stating, "They have no shot to do well on this test...." "They cannot pass this test...." I do not agree with these statements because they could lead to a negative mindset, which then could affect the way teachers prepare their students for this test.

As teachers, it is up to us to work hard so we can change the trend and reverse the numbers, while having a positive mindset. Although I am neither for nor against this test, I always make sure to stay positive about the experience. This enables my students to work hard on the test while not having to worry about the negativity surrounding it or things about the test that some people feel are unfair.

Year 4

After completing three solid school years at Riverhead Central School District, I was now confident teaching third grade. This school year, though, would prove to be the toughest. It was my fourth year of teaching, which meant, if I got through the year without any major problems or issues, I would receive tenure.

The school year in the classroom started off well. I was doing my best to motivate my students with daily inspirational speeches, etc. I also started to realize that I had a gift in teaching my students how to read and write, which was noticed early in the school year by an appreciative parent.

> Good morning,
> Thank you for the wonderful work you are doing with Sanku. Thank you for the writing samples that you send home with her so that we know what she needs help with, and most importantly, for us to see how great she is doing. She is a great little thinker! Her confidence is up, so it is nice to see her developing like that. We are so happy that you are her teacher. I just wanted to take a moment to let you know we appreciate it!
> Best,
> Palesa and Ketevi

As I was beginning to feel the weight of my tenure year, this email reassured me that what I was doing in the classroom was all that mattered. Looking back now, I know the confidence and inspiration I instilled in my students helped them to achieve lots of success that year. I saw many of my students make tremendous strides in reading and writing throughout the year. Furthermore, all the extra-help sessions during my lunch period and after school paid off for my students in math. I saw students who struggled to read and write at the beginning of the year prove their reading and writing skills by achieving high scores on the ELA Assessments and other assessments in the classroom.

Moreover, a few of my students who were labeled as "behavioral" students in second grade completed the school year as well-behaved students with no major issues in the classroom. I believe this is what happens when you have faith in your students and trust in them. My mother and father always told me to love my students and create relationships with them. My parents' wise advice has helped me to move mountains for my students.

As the year continued, the success continued. I prepared all my students for the NYS ELA Assessments, and again, my students proved that the test could not trick them or frustrate them, as they all performed at high levels. Furthermore, not one of my students who started the school year in my class opted out of the test. (Approximately 20% of students in NYS opt out each year, which is always a highly politicized issue before the test.) Most importantly, not one student acted out, got upset, or showed signs of stress throughout the entire two-day test.

Some feel the test is unfair for students, and I respect those opinions, but I do not worry about what is good or what is bad about the test. I just try to inspire my students and get them to have faith in themselves. I try to "train their brains" for weeks before the test, building their confidence and getting each student to actually enjoy doing the type of reading and writing that they will encounter on the test. "Practice makes better," which leads to joyful learning and removes the stress of performance. I also try to get the students to develop a different mindset. A mindset that trains their brains to think positively; a mindset that trains their brains to overcome. They were all very motivated and wanted to do well on the test.

My students had a class average of exactly 602 on the 2019 NYS ELA Assessments. (602 is the score in third grade that indicates level 3.) It was like my students were telling me right before I handed them the test: "Mr. Casamassa, hurry up reading the test directions and please give me the test. I can do it. I will overcome. Watch me persevere. I will do well and work hard on this test." It was as if I could see my students saying these things in their heads as I walked up and down the aisle before and during the test. How amazing they were.

I also had many students obtain a "high two" on the test that year. And since the students took the test in the beginning of April with one-fourth of the school year still left to go, I believe those students technically could be considered students who achieved their grade-level goals at that point in the year. To me, all of this data was amazing to analyze and humbling to experience as their teacher. If you get students to think positively and get them to believe that all things are possible in school and in life, they will experience tons of success.

As the school year came to a close, I had a weird feeling inside that my time at Riley Avenue School was coming to an end, even though my administrators always spoke highly of me. My students in all three of the years at Riley knew that I cared for them. And their parents supported me and knew what I was doing in the classroom for their children. I truly cared for my students and their families.

Toward the end of the year, my principal who told me minutes before that he loved me, called me into his office for a meeting to let me know that I was being transferred to another school in the district to teach first grade. I was devastated and heart broken. My assistant principal and the Assistant Superintendent of Schools also attended the meeting. I barely spoke during the meeting and just sat there, upset and devastated.

After a while, though, I decided to let things go and not fight the transfer anymore. My family told me to move on and not focus on the past even though I felt wronged.

Most importantly, that year ended successfully, as I earned my tenure. One thing was for sure in those four years: I did not care about vacations, summers off, etc. Those days off were never that important to me. I only cared about my students and their future success. My mother and father told me that if I wanted to become a teacher, then to do it for the right reasons. Each year in the classroom, I make sure to keep that in mind and only teach with a focus on my students. I am literally teaching the future of America.

Although I was sad to be leaving this school, at the end of the year, two parents showed their support and let the school district know how they felt about me. I was happy when I read their letters, which they Cc'd to my administration and superintendent.

Dear Mr. Casamassa,

I just wanted to thank you for a very wonderful year that my son Anthony had being in your class. Although he always had a great year with his past teachers at Riley, his year with you has been truly amazing. Thank you for making learning fun for him. I also would like to commend your approach in teaching the entire class throughout the year. Thank you for taking the time to help Anthony understand the lessons, especially in math. Anthony always comes home from school telling me great things that happened in class. He looks up to you and is very proud to tell everyone about you. You are very inspiring and such an awesome role model.

Although he is excited for summer, he is sad that his school year with you is ending. He actually told me in his own words that he will miss you as his teacher. Furthermore, I appreciate you always reaching out to let me know how Anthony was doing in class. I would not mind if Anthony could be in your class again if ever you will teach fourth grade. I am sure any Riley student (and their parents) would be grateful to be in your class.

You are an awesome addition amongst all the other members of the Riley faculty. Thank you for this amazing school year, and I hope you enjoy the summer. I look forward to bumping into you at school whenever I get a chance to volunteer, and I know Anthony will love seeing you in the hallways next year.

Best,
Marie

Lastly, shortly after being told I was getting transferred out of Riley, this letter lifted my spirits…

To Whom It May Concern:

I would like to nominate Mr. Daniel Casamassa as "Elementary Teacher of the Year" for the 2018-2019 school year. He is truly a hidden gem within Riverhead. My wife and I were blessed to have him teach our son. Mr. Casamassa is a humble teacher that stays away from the spotlight. Now is the time to showcase him to the district.

This year our son had Mr. Casamassa as his third grade teacher at Riley Avenue Elementary School. There was a lot of positive talk about him among the parents of former students. The parents raved about his positive reinforcement system, reward parties, ability to motivate unmotivated students, his fun teaching styles, positive energy, etc.

I also think Mr. Casamassa appealed to the children because he is young and has a lot of energy. My son wanted him as a teacher because he heard about some of the cool things he did in class. I also heard that he had a magical ability to work with "difficult" and "behavioral" students. My wife and I thought he would be a good fit for our son. Our son is intelligent but also strong-willed and not always easy to deal with. I remember the day Dylan received his teacher assignment in the mail. He was so excited that he was assigned to Mr. Casamassa's class. In my opinion, he had a lot of proving to do. Would he live up to the expectations that former students and parents alike created?

Throughout the course of the year, Dylan began to love school. He would eagerly talk about what he was learning. He would take it one step further and ask "Alexa" or "Siri" further questions about his school-related topics. He went from liking math to loving math. He enjoyed math so much that he asked us to buy math workbooks that he would work on for "fun." He began to enjoy writing and creating his own stories that he would work on at home. This motivation to do additional schoolwork was non-existent until this year with Mr. Casamassa.

Dylan started to dress up for school because he wanted to look nice like Mr. Casamassa. Not only did he want to dress nice, but he also wanted to behave well. He loved the reward system in Mr. Casamassa's class. He wanted to earn every possible reward sticker because he is a student that thrives on rewards, rather than punishments. As a reward, he earned "No Homework Passes" but chose not to use them because he wanted to do the work for Mr. Casamassa. Dylan also took his testing more seriously this year. He started to refer to his future and going to college.

Mr. Casamassa had a positive influence on Dylan's work ethic. This year Dylan took an interest in writing and reading. This was the first year that he asked for books for his birthday, Christmas, and Easter. One set of books he requested and read were the Harry Potter books. He also enjoyed bringing books home from Mr. Casamassa's personal library. Prior to third grade, reading was a tedious chore to him. This year Dylan became a rule follower. He always wanted to do everything right in front of Mr. Casamassa. Dylan did not like disappointing him. He did not want Mr. Casamassa to see him in a negative way and therefore made sure to follow his rules. Mr. Casamassa's teaching may be different from other teachers, however, it works! Not only does it work, it works well. His teaching style is something we should all embrace. He is truly about putting the students first.

My son is sad about moving up to fourth grade and saying goodbye to Mr. Casamassa. However, he is looking forward to visiting him and attending his "reunion" party next year. We are thankful he believed in our son. We are thankful that he helped our son strive to be the best that he can be.

We think Mr. Casamassa will be one of the teachers that our son will fondly remember, respect, and will look up to for many years to come. For all the work he has done this year, for putting the children first, working late hours, attending the students' sporting events, and initiating a spark in many students, I think Mr. Casamassa is very deserving to be "Elementary Teacher of the Year" for the 2018-2019 school year.

Sincerely,
Michael and Amy

I will save these letters forever but not to boast. Instead, I will save them to be reminded of what my past was like and how I was able to overcome challenges and create a future of hope and success because of hard work and perseverance. With the help of my parents and family, this was all possible. How amazing the journey has been.

Year 5

After getting transferred out of Riley Avenue School, I started the 2019-2020 school year off at Phillips Avenue School, teaching first grade. To begin the year, I will admit that I was still bitter and wanting to go back to the way my life was when it felt like everything was going well.

To get over what happened at Riley Avenue School, I had to move on even if it was not right or I was unfairly treated. Life is not always easy, so there was no reason to remain bitter about the situation. I had to do what I do best, which is teach my students with all my heart and all my soul. I had to inspire and motivate these students like my previous students, so they too can grow up to be the greatest police officers, the greatest doctors, the greatest farmers, lawyers, firemen, etc.

I will admit, I did not like teaching first grade initially, but as time went on, I regained my passion for teaching again, although it did take a few months. I had more ENL students in my class than the previous two years, but it did not matter. I was as focused as ever once the bitterness wore off, and I motivated and inspired those little six-year-olds to achieve greatness, just like I did for my former students.

In fact, when my principal observed me teaching in the classroom, she explained to me afterwards how she could tell how much my students looked up to me. My principal went on to say that she could tell my students loved and respected me. That gave me more motivation to continue pressing on during this difficult year of transition.

I saw my first graders grow as readers and writers. Many went from below grade level in reading to reaching grade level by the end of first grade. Another great accomplishment I achieved with my first graders was getting them all to write in real composition notebooks. One thing that I had a hard time dealing with as a first grade teacher was watching the students write on lined paper, which is simply a piece of paper with about five lines on it with a spot on the top of the paper to draw pictures.

I decided to take a gamble and give them all notebooks in December instead of using the "Kiddie Paper," which is what my students and I called the lined paper. The gamble paid off, and in no time, my students were writing in paragraph form, while indenting with capital letters and punctuation marks in actual notebooks. That school year taught me to never underestimate my students, no matter how young they are. All students are capable to learn anything through hard work and perseverance. My first graders were certainly a testament to that. I will miss them dearly.

Along with many other great experiences I had teaching first grade, there were two in particular that stood out. The first experience was with one of my students. His name is Avery. He was labeled as a "behavioral" student in kindergarten. He was considered a "high-profile" student coming up to first grade. I heard stories about Avery and what he had supposedly done in his kindergarten class. All I heard was, "Avery did this…," "Avery did that…" Teachers were telling me that security had to be called down to his classroom every day to remove him. After hearing all the chatter, I was even more eager to teach him in first grade.

To be honest, when Avery arrived in my class in September, it was a struggle. I consider myself a patient teacher, but I had no patience to begin that year because I was still upset about my transfer out of third grade. I believe this caused Avery to continue his social struggles to begin first grade. Each day people were asking me how Avery was doing. Even though he was struggling to begin the year, I always told them that he was "doing well." I did that because I am a very positive teacher and knew he would be just fine in the end.

As time went on and our relationship grew stronger, his behavior drastically improved. Gone were the days of hitting staff members and others. Gone were the days of temper tantrums. Avery turned into a leader. A leader that helped his classmates out when they were in need. A leader who respected me and his peers. Moreover, Avery was always quick to ask me for help when I was in need, and he even filled up my water cup every time I was low on water. I was so proud of him.

This was a student who some in that school thought should be sent to "BOCES." I knew BOCES all too well, and to be honest, I had doubts at first when he joined my class. Then I quickly remembered what I went through and my troubled past and worked with Avery more and more and he started to trust me, and in turn, respect and listen to me. I build a relationship with him. Avery, along with my other first graders, I know are destined for greatness and a future of hope.

During that school year, there was also a one-on-one conversation I had with one of my students that really inspired me. When I had this student in first grade, he was a superstar from day 1. He respected me, worked hard every day, and never stopped persevering. He was one of my ENL students, but you would never know it if you walked into my classroom, as he was always attentive and focused on the task at hand. He also started the school year reading A/B level books and finished the school year reading H books, which is where first graders should be at the end of the school year.

One of the unique ways that I connect with my students is by having one-on-one conversations about life with them. I ask them about their lives, what they want to be when they are older, etc. At the end of my "life" conversation with this student after asking him what he wanted to be when he grows up, he replied back: "Mr. Casamassa, when I grow up, I want to be an astronaut. I want to go to the Moon one day. And when I get to the Moon, I will take some rocks and bring them back and give them to you. If I do not become an astronaut, I want to be a teacher like you."

Some days are very stressful as a teacher, but when I hear things like that from my students, it gives me strength. This student was truly amazing. I cannot wait to see what he is going to accomplish in the future. I also cannot wait to see what all my other first graders will become when they are older. A lot of them told me that they wanted to be a teacher when they are older. Whenever one of them told me that, I just responded and said, "Yea, that is great you want to be a teacher. I am sure you will grow up to be one of the greatest teachers out there. In fact, I know you will."

First grade might not have been my favorite grade to teach, but one thing was for sure: Those first graders were loved just like all my past students were loved. They were treated the same. They were respected the same. And most of all, they were motivated and inspired in the same exact way as my former students.

This school year proved to be bittersweet because school was shut down in March due to the COVID-19 pandemic. Although it was quite difficult and depressing teaching from home each day from March until June, I still found a way to find the beauty in the shutdown. Because of the fact that a lot of my students did not have technological devices and/or internet access at home, I decided to buy my students 15 books each, so they could easily work on their reading skills without having to worry about accessing the internet, etc.

Furthermore, to make sure each student received their books, I drove to their homes and dropped the books into their mailboxes.

What filled me with even more joy during this time was having my students read their new books to me over the phone once a week for 20 minutes. This way of teaching was obviously not as good as teaching them in person, but it proved to be effective because I had the same books that they had right in front of me, which allowed me to help them with pronunciation, comprehension, etc. This was the highlight of my week during the shutdown and the best way I could finish up a roller coaster school year.

Throughout my first few years of teaching, not only do I repeat in my mind particular quotes each day to motivate myself and help me get through the struggles of work and life, I make sure to proclaim them out loud to my students so they could also live by them. Here are some of those inspirational quotes, which I declare to my students on a daily basis: always choose kind; your future is bright like the stars; work before play; patience is a virtue; reading is thinking; if you study, you don't need luck; choose a positive mindset; no one is perfect; everyone is going through a struggle; hard work leads to success; persevere and never give up.

And finally, not only do I enjoy expressing the above quotes each day to my students, I also enjoy writing a letter to my class each morning, which I display on the SMART Board as part of the "morning message." To get a better idea of my teaching style and the motivation that I try to instill in my students through these writings, below is a letter that I wrote to my fifth-grade students one morning during the 2020-2021 school year.

April 6, 2021

> Dear Boys and Girls,
> Please unpack and do your morning work quietly. Complete page 202 in your workbooks. Today you have gym class at 8:25. As I mentioned yesterday, you all looked a bit tired, but I thought you did a nice job fighting through the tiredness, as it was the first day back from spring break. Furthermore, please continue to persevere on your journey to a higher reading level. It will all be worth it in the end. A lot of people say that "teaching is a hard job." And then I think to myself, "Yes, it is, but many jobs are hard." I believe that my job is easier

because of you. It's so easy to teach because you are always showing me respect, never giving up, etc. From now on, when people ask me if I have a good class or not, I will reply back to them: "I don't have a good class; I have a great class!" **Quote of the day**: "A negative mind will never give you a positive life." And always remember: Bullying is never the answer. Have a wonderful day!

Sincerely,
Mr. Casamassa

After getting through five full years of teaching in Riverhead, I feel more blessed than ever before. As you already know, I taught sixth grade my first year, third grade the next three years, then first grade. I am still working in the Riverhead Central School District and presently teaching fifth grade. Teaching fifth grade has been a unique experience, as eight of my 23 students were in my third grade class from two years ago, the year I was transferred. It is funny how things always work out in the end.

Besides this unique experience, all my fifth graders have been truly a blessing to me and have helped me get through this school year, especially with all the new restrictions and rules that have been mandated due to the COVID-19 pandemic. (See chapter nine to learn more about my amazing fifth graders and the overflowing amount of faith and optimism they have had during the 2020-2021 school year.)

The experiences of teaching in all these different grades have been amazing, and I cannot believe what my students have accomplished. I pray for my students every day, and God answers my prayers. I persevere with my students each day, and God perseveres with me. I love my students, and He is there continuing to love me. How amazing!

An Inspirational Quote for You

"Tell me and I forget. Teach me and I remember. Involve me and I learn."

—Benjamin Franklin

Throughout all my teaching experiences thus far, I have made sure to involve my students every day and keep them motivated. I believe this has been the key to their success. Whether it is the videos or pictures I show them in science and social studies, the math lessons that I relate to real life, or even the reading and writing lessons that are filled with passion to read and write on a high level, motivating my students is always my number one goal. If I can get all my students to actually enjoy coming to school, then the battle of staying engaged and learning will be that much easier.

NINE

The Power of Faith

As you have read so far, hard work, perseverance, and faith were the driving forces that helped me overcome all the obstacles that I faced in my past. Though I had doubts at different times in my life, I always stayed optimistic and faithful. I was persistent and refused to fail.

In high school I could have easily given up. The thought of dropping out from school was continuously running through my mind. I felt as if someone was telling me to walk away and another person was telling me to not give up; it was good versus evil.

When I was in high school, my father would write encouraging letters to me on a weekly basis. Rereading those letters recently brought back sad memories when I was at a low point in life. The thoughts in my head at the time were all negative, as I was thinking about giving up in school. The letters back then did prove one thing to me, though: My parents loved me and refused to let me give up. On the next page is one of those letters.

Dan,

Thank you for keeping the agreement for the 3 days even if it was one sided. I want to see you go out but I want you to be responsible, not just for your mother & I but for yourself as well. Be disciplined in what you do and it will always be a help to you in the future. We want you home at night, no later than 12:45 AM, thats very reasonable! Show us that you are willing to do that consistantly and we will extend it to a later time. We love you and we want to see you succeed, young people don't want to be restricted, however it is for their benefit that they are. I'll be praying for the job, I want to see you get a car and to be independant so that you can start doing things on your own. You need to save money and to make it a habit. Don't shun our advice, your mom and I have both been there and we know how it is. Without money it is very hard to do a lot of things. I told you once and I haven't forgotten, every dollar that you save for a car I will match, thats between you and me and not for the rest of the family to know. I want to see you be a leader and not a follower, there is a lot of loosers out there. A smart person is one who will listen to others who have be successful so that they can learn from them. Coach K didn't become great over night, he learned from others, look on the bench next to him and see former players learning how to coach you will see them one day coaching a team of their own. Be careful on the outside there is a lot of stuff that can hurt you and a lot of people who will help you find it because they are lost and want company. Be wise and think about what you are doing, it will stay with you for the rest of your life. I love you even though you didnt appreciate my tough love tactics recently, work with me, you would be surprised and what we could do for each other

Love Dad

It was like I could see the tears dripping down onto the paper from my father's eyes. That letter was during my trying times in high school. After all the trouble and agony, the sad letters from my father turned into letters filled with tears of joy.

Dan,

When I got home last night I went upstairs but remembered that I still had wash downstairs. I was trying to figure out when I would go down to put them in the dryer. All of a sudden I looked at the bed I saw my pants that I really wanted to be cleaned, it took me a moment to understand that my wonderful son had finished the job for me, for which I am very greatful. Thank you so much, you're amazing, God bless you.

Love
Dad

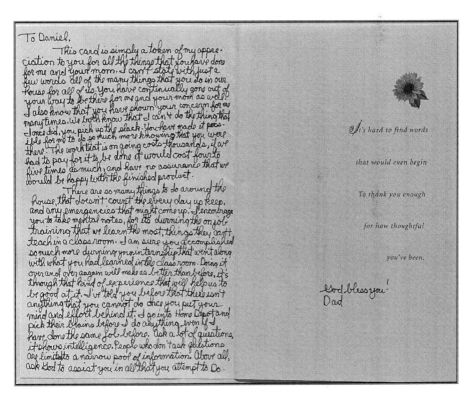

To Daniel,

This card is simply a token of my appreciation to you for all the things that you have done for me and your mom. I can't state with just a few words all of the many things that you do in our house for all of us. You have continually gone out of your way to be there for me and your mom as well. I also know that you have shown your concern for me many times. We both know that I can't do the things that I once did, you pick up the slack. You have made it possible for me to do so much more knowing that you were there. The work that is on going costs thousands, if we had to pay for it to be done it would cost four to five times as much, and have no assurance that we would be happy with the finished product.

There are so many things to do around the house, that doesn't count the every day up keep, and any emergencies that might come up. I encourage you to take mental notes, for it's durning the on job training that we learn the most, things they can't teach in a class room. I am sure you accomplished so much more durning your internship that went along with what you had learned in the class room. Doing it over and over again will make us better than before, it's through that kind of experience that will help us to be good at it. I've told you before that there isn't anything that you cannot do once you put your mind and effort behind it. I go into Home Depot and pick their brains before I do anything, even if I have done the same job before. Ask a lot of questions, it shows intelligence. People who don't ask questions are limited to a narrow pool of information. Above all, ask God to assist you in all that you attempt to do.

It's hard to find words

that would even begin

To thank you enough

for how thoughtful

you've been.

God bless you!
Dad

Hi Dan,

This is the day that the Lord has made, rejoice and be glad in it. Dan, I am a witness of all the hard work that has gone on in leading up to this day, the first day of your teaching career. You have proved so many wrong, and have over come so much, which traslates into, if God is for you who can be against you. I just finished praying for you and will continue to do so through out the day. Remember, your not just a teacher. You are a mighty man of God, and you are a hero to these kids, they will remember you all the days of their lives. You can make a tremendous impact in their young lives, that will help them in making the right decisions beyond what you are teaching them. Pray each day for them and pray a blood line (of Christ) around them and the class room, for their protection and yours. The enemy wants to destroy the work of God and so we need to be in spiritual warfare at all times, in prayer call for God's power and ability to bless those kids that He has given to you for ministry. Have a nice weekend, please pray for your mom and I to hear from God over the weekend. If you go to church on Sun., please pick up about 75 of the play post cards and if the tickets are available please get as many as you can get, I think you can get 9 for each of the 6 presentations. I need more than that but do the best that you can. I love you and your mom and I are very proud of you, you are truly a miracle of God. God bless you

Love Dad

My father knew the potential I had, and it frustrated him to see me not living up to my full potential. He kept writing to me and hoping that one day something would click inside of me. It was quite simple: My father was optimistic and had faith in me. The letters of love and encouragement slowly helped me gain confidence and realize that my father was actually not against me but clearly in my corner.

The dictionary says that faith is simply a "complete trust or confidence in something or someone." I believe we all need to have at least some faith in something or someone because if we lack faith, we are lacking true belief in life. Faith brings optimism, and optimism brings positive results. The positive results that you obtain will then breed confidence, and in turn, your confidence will help to produce success. This cycle is one that I follow in my life. And as a teacher, this is a cycle I try to always instill in my students, which helps them to have faith in themselves: faith that is unending and strong.

I try to be optimistic in life and stay faithful each and every day, although I admit, it is difficult. I try to "walk by faith and not by sight." My faith has made me the man I am today, and the optimistic mindset that I have helps me to stay strong during the tough times. It is hard at times to stay faithful because of the simple fact that it entails believing in something that we cannot see. This is why we need to have an optimistic mindset in order to strengthen our faith, which will help to minimize the doubts in life. This type of faith is what I call "optimistic faith."

Optimistic Faith at Its Finest

The 2017 Superbowl is one of the greatest examples why it is important to stay optimistic and faithful, even when things look hopeless. In the 2017 Superbowl, The New England Patriots were down 21-3 at halftime to the Atlanta Falcons. They were also down 28-3 with 8:32 remaining in the third quarter. Up to that point in the game, the Superbowl, which is the most-watched event in America, turned into the most unwatchable event. That was until The Patriots, led by Tom Brady, Julian Edelman, and others, stormed back late in the third quarter.

At halftime, Tom Brady and Julian Edelman were sitting by themselves on the bench, looking toward the field in silence. Then, Julian Edelman breaks the silence: "Let's go, baby. It's gonna be a hell of a story." Tom Brady calmly and confidently responds, "Hell yea." I cannot tell you how many times I watched that video clip to pump me up. You could see just by the look in their eyes and the determination on their faces that they literally believed they would come back and win the Superbowl.

The Patriots eventually forced overtime and won the game 34-28. This was and still is the greatest comeback in Superbowl history. There are other sound bites from that game, specifically in the second half, where Julian Edelman is once again showing his faith in the huddle, saying to his teammates, "You gotta believe!"

I truly believe the Patriots came back in that game not because of their athletic ability or talent, but rather due to their faith and belief in themselves. They stayed positive during the tough parts of the game and eventually achieved their goal. This is a lesson that teaches us to always stay faithful, optimistic, and of course, never give up!

Example #2

The next lesson learned is about a student I taught in third grade during the 2016-2017 school year. Her name is Jessie-Ann. She came into my classroom below grade level in reading, writing, and math. She was a quiet student, so I made sure to motivate her as best as I could. Most importantly, I always told her to continue to believe and stay positive, which was the turning point.

Little by little, Jessie-Ann started to grow in each subject area, especially in reading and writing. Furthermore, I provided her with direct instruction during many extra-help sessions at lunchtime and even after school with a few other students. This strategy proved to be the difference maker because as the year continued, her reading level increased dramatically. I made sure to provide regular updates to her mother about how much her daughter was flourishing in school.

In April of that school year, I administered the NYS ELA Assessments to my students. Jessie-Ann took a long time to complete the test, but she worked extremely hard and persevered the entire time. In fact, she worked so hard that I had to collect her test so she could take a break to eat lunch and then continue the test in the afternoon. She wanted to do well on the test, and finishing the test completely was important to her. It was important to me as well, regardless of the score she would receive.

Finally, after working on the test during two different parts of the school day, Jessie-Ann handed in her test. I told her how proud I was that she continued the test without giving up.

At the end of the summer, I received the test scores for my students. All of my students performed extremely well on the test, including Jessie-Ann who did amazing and scored a 3 on the test!

Some might feel this test is too hard for students like Jessie-Ann that receive extra help in reading, ENL, or another subject, but I always try to be optimistic and believe that these students can perform just as well as their peers. I believe that because Jessie-Ann had an optimistic mindset and was faithful, she was able to perform at a high level in my class. I had faith in Jessie-Ann, and she had faith in me and knew that I was going to be there to support and motivate her during the tough times.

Not only did Jessie-Ann believe in me, but her mother also had faith in me. I ran into Jessie-Ann's mother a few months after the school year ended, and she expressed to me how much she appreciated the extra attention and help that I gave to her daughter. Her mother went on in this conversation to tell me that Jessie-Ann actually "wanted to take the test." This is another great example why it is important to always stay positive. and faithful during times of difficulty.

Example #3

My first year teaching fifth grade in the 2020-2021 school year was interesting, to say the least. My students and I were required to wear masks in the classroom all year long, while also practicing social distancing to combat the COVID-19 pandemic.

Before the school year began, my school district had to decide whether or not to send students back to school in September for normal instruction or start the year with virtual learning five days per week. After many meetings and discussions, my school district decided to have students attend school in person to begin the year. The plan was to split the students in each class into cohorts. Cohort one attended on Mondays and Tuesdays, and the second cohort attended on Thursdays and Fridays. Wednesday was designated as a cleaning day.

Many teachers were skeptical at the decision to bring students back into the classroom to begin the school year. Personally, I tried to stay away from the politics of the decision, so I could focus on my students and teach them with all my heart and soul. Even with all the new restrictions due to the pandemic, I was extremely happy to see my students in September. Despite the uncertainty, after a few weeks in school things were going well. Against all odds, we did not have many positive COVID-19 cases, and my school district continued to stay open.

Although many believed we would shut down after just a "few weeks," I had faith we would stay open. Not only did September go well, the first few weeks of October went just as well, as my school district continued to stay open for business.

Then all of a sudden toward the end of October, my school district was in the "yellow zone" and labeled a "micro-cluster," as it had one of the highest COVID-19 positivity rates on Long Island. A number of staff members tested positive for the disease, so for two weeks all students in the district were taught online.

Eventually, my district fought off the "micro-cluster" label, and the positivity rate for COVID-19 declined in our schools. This allowed us to continue educating our students in school, instead of having to teach them from home. In fact, not only did my school district stay open after the Christmas break, but we also did away with the two cohorts and went back full-time starting on January 11, 2021. This meant class sizes were back to normal (approximately 25 students per class) and that students could once again attend school every day.

Through all the uncertainty, those at the top of my school district leading the way stayed faithful and optimistic. They stayed calm through all the noise. Moreover, I had so much faith and optimism that we would continue to stay open, so I instructed my students to keep their school laptops in the classroom. (We were told to have our students take home their school laptops each day after school in case of an unexpected shutdown.) I just knew in my heart that this would not happen, and thankfully, it never did.

The optimistic faith that my students and I showed in room 214 at Pulaski Street School in the Riverhead Central School District during the 2020-2021 school year was an example of faith that I will never forget. An optimistic mindset will always overpower a pessimistic one, and faith will always win out over doubt. My amazing fifth graders certainly proved this to be true.

I hope the three examples above will encourage you to always stay optimistic and faithful. The one who gives up displays hopelessness, but the one who shows determination and fight, will reap the benefits of their unflappable faith. Think positively and never give up!

<u>An Inspirational Quote for You</u>

"Feed your faith and your doubts will starve to death."
– Gaur Gopal Das

I never gave up in school even though I had thoughts of doing so. I kept pressing on when I needed to and fought the battles that I had to. If you want to be successful in life, then you have to overcome the trouble that is bound to come your way with a faithful mindset. Do not give up after one or two tries, or even after fifty tries. Give up only if the clock runs out. Until then, your effort, hard work, and faith will be key contributors to how successful you will be.

TEN

Wonder

During the course of writing this book, I began to feel more at peace with my life and what I have accomplished thus far. For whatever reason, I felt many "chains" of my past were now broken, and I could finally live in the present and look toward the future without any regrets.

I have started looking at the things around me more, specifically this amazing planet that we are living on, and I am truly in awe at what I see. Whether it is the wonder of the mountains from a distance, or the oceans, lakes, and rivers, I think about this planet, the only planet with life, and I just smile.

Once in a while, I like to go outside at night by myself and enjoy the cool breeze, while observing the wonders of the Moon and its brightness alongside the stars. Even though I already know the answers in my heart and mind to many of the following questions, I still like to reflect on life and ask myself: How did we end up on Planet Earth? How was a man able to actually walk on the Moon? How does my body continue to work and function properly each and every day? Why was I put here on Earth? When will this wonderful life end?

These questions and more are important for all of us to reflect on as they force us to take on a different perspective. This perspective could help us be more grateful for this amazing life that we are living and all the gifts and blessings we have had, especially living in this beautiful country. Hopefully the poems on the next few pages will give you a better understanding of how I truly feel about life.

Planet Earth

Planet Earth, Planet Earth, how amazing you are
Planet Earth, Planet Earth, so close but so far.
The Sun, Moon, and stars brighten you each day
Whether snow in December or flowers in May.

You bring all the seasons just because of your tilt
How beautiful you are, how strong you are built.
God spins you around the Sun once a year
He also rotates you daily without no fear.

Thanks for your wonder, thanks for your beauty
You give us the ability to breathe and live freely.
I will never take for granted to live amongst your splendor
You're the only planet with life, so peaceful and tender.

My Life

Dear life, you're so amazing but why all the heartache?
I pray it will go away each morning I awake.
Loved ones come and go but you're always unchanged
It seems unfair, so confusing and deranged.

But then I think about all the years I've endured thus far
And I thank you for them as I'm still in awe.
I made it through my mother's womb and childhood as well
I also made it through the school years barely able to spell.

Now that I'm teaching and have achieved much success
I thank you for all the ups and downs as I passed those tests.
But remember who made you a long time ago
And remember to thank Him before it's time to go.

My Students

My students, my students, how awesome they are
My students, my students, destined to go far.
They sit at their desks just hoping and waiting
For that one special moment, that knowledge for the taking.

They are wonderful like the stars shining at night
They read and write nonstop with no end in sight.
Police officers, doctors, farmers they will be
These are my students, bright futures I see.

Motivation and inspiration are two things I give them
So they can obtain success and shine like a gem.
Their smiles, their laughter bring me such happiness
I'm honored to teach them, I'm definitely blessed.

My Family

My family, my family, so much love it's overflowing
We are the greatest family ever without even knowing.
They gave me hope when all hope was lost
Blood, sweat, and tears no matter the cost.

Through fights and arguments, our love never wavered
For that we give thanks to our Lord and Savior.
He kept us so strong through heartache and tragedy
And just like a fairy tale, our story will end happily.

Let's do it for my father, our Grandma, and all those we've lost
Let's do it for the one who died on the cross.
There is nothing we can't accomplish, nothing we can't do
So let's keep reaching greatness, spreading love like we do.

<u>Let Us Pray</u>

Lord, I want to thank you for the many gifts you have given us in life. I thank you for your masterpiece (Planet Earth) and placing everything in its correct place to sustain so much through thousands of years of existence. Even though we are all going through some type of struggle in life, we still praise you for simply giving us air to breathe and a beautiful life to live. We thank you for family and friends that console us during tough times. We also thank you for helping us to persevere and get through the tragedies and heartaches of life. Life certainly can be tough at times, but you have proven to be much tougher as you fight through the struggles with us. We do remember, though, that you went through the worst kind of struggle being crucified on the cross. And although it was heartbreaking to watch, it essentially gave us this life to live thousands of years later. We thank you for dying just so that we could live. How unselfish you are. Finally, we thank you for always forgiving us even though we do not deserve it. The forgiveness you give us daily should remind us that we always need to "forgive those who trespass against us." If not, then why should we expect your forgiveness when we do something wrong? You are so wonderful. Please, Lord, continue to do amazing things in our lives. Continue to bless this amazing country that we are living in, no matter who our president is. And continue to bless your creation, Planet Earth, for many more generations to come. In your name we pray, amen.

An Inspirational Quote for You

"Think of all the beauty still left around you and be happy."
– Anne Frank

Anne Frank wrote this quote in 1944 while she and her family were hiding from the Nazis in Germany. She still was able to see the beauty and wonder in the world, even with all the hate and sorrow that was surrounding her and other Jews at the time. I think we should heed Anne Frank's advice. Every once in a while, do yourself a favor and observe the beautiful features of our planet. Whether it is the changing of the seasons, the planets, the animals, or all the various landscapes, make an effort to enjoy the unique attributes of Earth before your life is over, as it is truly something beautiful to take in.

AFTERWORD

Well, that is my story up to age 36. All the accounts in this book are true and written for one purpose only: to show that through hard work and perseverance, all things are possible. My rough past is behind me, and I am now trying to take life one day at a time. Thanks to the support of my loving family, I am creating a bright future for myself, my students, and helping people out whenever I can.

If you are still living at home with your parents, please, listen to your parents and obey their rules. Your parents are the ones buying the clothes you are wearing and the food you are eating, so respect them because you never know when they will be gone forever, and you do not want to live with regrets the rest of your life.

I am a person that continues to live life through a process of change, like all of us are doing. Change for me was hard to deal with and still is, but as I mature and grow more emotionally and intellectually, change will continue to be easier to cope with. I am also a more loving person than I was in the past and accept help more often. I sin and make mistakes just like everyone else does, but I try to be quick when seeking forgiveness.

I am glad that I was able to pay people back for my past transgressions and wrongdoings. For example, I made sure to pay back my family members and others whom I had done wrong to financially in the past. I try to give back and help them out whenever I can, especially for all their sacrifice through the years.

As for my academic deficiencies, they still make it tough for me to read, and even teach at times. But I continue to learn new things and work hard every day, so I do not lose focus academically, especially while teaching. God has given me strength in weakness and power to overcome. In the Bible, Philippians 4:13 states: "I can do all things through Christ who strengthens me." I recite this verse every day, so I can be reminded of who helped me beat the odds and overcome the trials I faced. Now I am an overcomer.

I believe with time and some faith you too will overcome your troubles. Wouldn't it be nice to one day call yourself overcomer? I hope in your life you take some of the steps that I took to fight through the adversity. Whether it was being diagnosed with a disability, getting left back, or feeling depressed, I kept pressing on, while following a three-step approach: Work hard, have faith, and never give up!

Fun Facts About the Author

1. Favorite television shows: Live PD, Shark Tank, and The First 48
2. Before I became a teacher, I always wanted to be a police officer.
3. I became a vegan in 2020.
4. I have to shave every day.
5. I have never taken a sick or personal day from work (six years and counting).
6. Someone once bet me $100 to do 1,000 push-ups in an hour, which I completed with just minutes to spare.
7. A co-worker once bet me $100 that I could not eat an entire pizza pie in an hour....I won the bet with just seconds remaining!
8. I do 500 pushups a day.
9. I cannot wear a pair of pants or a shirt unless it is ironed.
10. When school was closed down due to the COVID-19 pandemic, I taught myself how to speak Spanish.
11. I still use a BlackBerry cellphone.
12. I am left-handed.
13. I have never received stitches or broken a bone.
14. I have never had a credit card.
15. My favorite subject to teach is writing.
16. I never use a microwave to cook or to heat up food.
17. I eat salad with a spoon.
18. I do not eat dinner until 9:00 p.m.
19. My "junk drawer" is very neat and organized.
20. After text messaging with someone, I have to delete the conversation.

Made in the USA
Middletown, DE
26 July 2021